Everything You Thought About Marketing
Your Plastic Surgery Practice Is Wrong

Plastic Surgery
Marketing On The
Internet

Attract MORE PATIENTS Than

You Can Handle and DOUBLE

YOUR PROFITS In Half The Time

Marc Savage

D1229377

Published by Hypnotic Media, LLC

Printed in the United States of America.

ISBN: 978-0-9905873-0-9

Dedication

To the many physicians and plastic surgeons that want to build practices and provide for your families. Now is the time to invest in your financial and professional success.

Table of Contents

The Marketing Imperative!

"Relying too much on proof distracts you from the real mission...Selling to people who actually want to hear from you is more effective than interrupting strangers who don't."

– Seth Godin

To everyone who has ever deleted emails without opening them, raged about telemarketers who call during dinner, tossed "junk mail" in the garbage with no more than a cursory glance, or run to the kitchen for a snack during a commercial break, I wrote this book for you. I wrote it because there is a better way to get your message in front of people actively seeking a plastic surgeon. Of course, getting seen is only part of the challenge. They will only become your patients when they feel you have their interests at heart—when you make a strong emotional connection. That process is the subject of this book.

While it may seem easy to write off marketing and advertising as the sole purview of Mad Men, silver-tongued pitchmen and modern-day sellers of snake oil—and beneath the professionalism of a physician—there's a reason companies

1

worldwide spend close to $1 trillion a year to promote their products and services. Somebody's opening those emails; buying from telemarketers; responding to the myriad postcards, letters and flyers that arrive in the mail; and watching commercials. Sometimes it's even you. But "sometimes" isn't good enough odds.

What's Wrong with Marketing?

Most traditional marketing has been a crapshoot. *First*, the messages don't reach us at the exact moment when we are ready to buy, at least not with any regularity. Such imprecision leaves companies no choice but to play the numbers games, called volume and frequency. Mail goes out in bulk and commercials have to run regularly if companies are going to catch enough people who happen to be ready to buy, but even then, they have to be satisfied with small, single-digit response rates. As a return on investment (ROI) that's abysmal.

Second, most marketing messages are pushed on us. We can't read a magazine, watch television, pick up our mail, or listen to the radio without being pitched. In any 24-hour period, we are bombarded with hundreds, if not thousands, of commercial messages. It's called interruption marketing because it intrudes in our lives whether or not we're interested or receptive. Companies send out their marketing messages on their schedule, not ours—a huge mistake. More often, it's the interruption, not the message that sends us running from the room during commercial breaks, hanging up on telemarketers, and chucking our unread junk mail (both digital and printed).

But all that changes when we're ready to purchase. When we're in control of the process and schedule, we go searching for information. Because no one wants to make an uninformed decision, we're willing to spend hours on research...scanning the

2

newspapers for a local sale, visiting merchant and manufacturing sites on social media, and reading product reviews on Amazon. But what we're most likely to do is run an online search—what we call "Googling" whether we are using Google, Bing, Yahoo! or any of a dozen other popular search engines. Depending on the study you read, anywhere from 78 percent to 90 percent of all buying decisions begin with search.

So no, it's not the marketing that we hate; it's the unsolicited delivery that drives us crazy. <u>And in that distinction lays the secret to your successful marketing campaign.</u> It's possible today to reach prospective patients at the exact moment when they want to find a local plastic surgeon to perform a rhinoplasty, augmentation mammaplasty, hair transplantation, Botox, or any of the many surgical procedures or minimally invasive treatments you offer.

The Sea Change in Marketing

Until very recently, the effectiveness of marketing and advertising campaigns has been taken more or less on faith. But with the advent of the Internet and digital tracking tools, that's been slowly changing. Corporate management today is requiring greater accountability of their marketing departments and proof that their marketing campaigns are delivering a respectable return on investment.

With the ability to track, the expectations and demands being put on marketing are truly industry changing. Case in point, a 2012 report noted that 1.8 trillion display ads had been paid for but never seen by their intended audiences. So egregious was this lost opportunity that the Interactive Advertising Bureau issued its Making Measurement Make Sense initiative and demanded that advertisers receive better results. This has required several technical changes to digital display advertising

3

systems, but two years later improvements are being measured and noted. More money than ever is pouring into digital advertising—across all platforms and forms of advertising. Marketing research firm eMarketer reports a global **digital** ad spend of $137.53 billion in 2014. That's up more than 14 percent from 2013 and accounts for a quarter of all paid media spending worldwide. Better testing and tracking and the ability to tweak messages in a digital format is drawing dollars from traditional advertising media and redirecting them to the Internet.

While change is occurring fastest in the large, global corporations, the evidence that we can all do a better job both of tracking results and targeting prospective customers is trickling down to even the smallest Internet businesses. In short, digital is changing the way we all work online to promote our businesses. One interesting caveat in all this: While I say all, it is companies (those with the marketing budgets) that have been quicker to realize the advantages of digital advertising and marketing than their agencies. Companies recognize the need to focus on results (ROI), while agencies have been slow to see beyond the traditional media buy. With the growing demand for accountability and return on investment, agencies will either adjust or disappear. We'll being discussing the market, message and media (and their order of importance) throughout this book because they represent the difference between marketing "on a wing and a prayer" and building a highly targeted campaign that's fully optimized to deliver the greatest possible ROI.

I wrote this book because that change is not restricted to companies with the luxury of multi-million dollar marketing budgets. Small businesses and local service providers are learning to use the Internet more effectively—to target their messages, to take advantage of cost-effective analytical tools, and to reach their best prospects. Professional practices can do the same. No one can afford to drag the sea of potential prospects with the

4

marketing equivalent of a fishing trawler's net in the vague hope of scooping up enough clients and patients to justify the expenditure. We've entered an era of smart, customer-centric marketing, which means you need to give your best prospects the right tools and information to make a buying decision. The practices that do it best—with a program optimized for success—will win. It is that simple.

A Better Way to Play the Game

If you read any of the Internet marketing articles aimed at smaller businesses and professional practices, you may be tempted to try your hand at reaching prospective patients by using many of the free tools and marketing platforms available. You may be blogging, posting on social media sites and relying on search engine optimization (SEO) to put yourself and your practice in front of your target audience. Or you may be thinking about it.

As I'll explain when we get to the section of the book on Traffic, blogging, social media and SEO all have their place. But these are secondary strategies because even though the tools are free, they require significant time and energy to build an online presence that stands out. Not only that, you'll spend countless hours keeping up with changes in the SEO rules and expanding your participation to the new social platforms that keep cropping up.

If you want fast results, and who doesn't, you need to use Paid Search. It's affordable, and you control exactly how much you spend on every campaign. Even more important, Paid Search puts your promotional message in front of prospective patients with surgical precision—exactly at the time when they are looking for the procedures and treatments you have to offer.

If you're wondering how this works, you'll connect with people on the front page of their search results through a Pay Per Click (PPC) ad. PPC is a powerful tool in it's own right. Since 1996, companies have relied on Paid Search—using keywords to match their ads with specific Internet search requests.

But this is not just another book about Pay Per Click. PPC is only a small piece of the Emotional Direct Response Marketing techniques I'm bringing to you. Emotional Direct Response Marketing is a comprehensive marketing strategy built to optimize each component of your marketing campaign for maximum results. It's not enough to post a PPC ad and hope for good clickthrough rates. It's not enough to send prospects to your website and assume they'll find the information they need and will like what they see about you. And it's not enough to post your phone number, then sit back and wait for the business to roll in.

When you optimize the components of a marketing campaign, you are thinking about how to pre-sell your services and abilities. And this takes both decisions and understanding on your part. It's not a long, drawn out process. But it does demand focus. You need to understand the customer (in your case, the patient). Who she is...who he is? What do they need to hear from you? What will resonate and show that you understand? What's the ideal way to encourage a prospective patient to take the next step toward becoming your patient? Think of all this as a way to bring good bedside manner to the Internet. And once the components are built and working together, you will have a system that runs virtually on autopilot for as long as you want...with a minimum of effort spent monitoring, analyzing and tweaking for maximum results.

Emotional Direct Response Marketing is the difference between running a few ads that direct people to your plastic surgery website, and crafting a customer-focused campaign that

6

invites prospective patients to follow a series of steps that speak directly to their wants and needs. At each stage, by providing the right information needed to make an informed buying decision—with just the right tone—an Emotional Direct Response Marketing campaign helps prospects qualify themselves. They decide if a procedure is right for them. They decide if you are the right doctor. By the time they are in your office for a consultation, you can have prospects pre-sold and primarily interested in meeting the doctor who will perform their procedure.

The Internet has turned traditional marketing on its head. It has put our customers, clients and even patients in charge of the buying process. Emotional Direct Response Marketing enables you to fulfill their expectations with an automated system that delivers your message to people who are actively looking for a plastic surgeon and gives them the informational tools to make a decision to buy from you. And you can do this while controlling what you spend.

It's time you put 21ˢᵗ-century marketing to work for your practice.

- Marc Savage

Introduction

Stop Offering Services!
Market for Success!

"The aim of marketing is to know and understand the customer so well the product or service fits him and sells itself."

– Peter Drucker

W hether it's our celebrity-obsessed culture, the aging population, increased time in the sun, the popularity of television shows like *Nip/Tuck* and *Dr. 90210*, the many advances in minimally invasive technologies, or all of the above, plastic surgery—and specifically cosmetic procedures—has been on the fast track for at least the past decade. According to the American Society of Plastic Surgeons, in 2005 Americans had 10.2 million cosmetic procedures. Today this $14-plus billion industry accounts for more than 15 million cosmetic procedures annually.

So, how's this growth trend benefiting your practice? Are you satisfied with the results? Are you reaching your best market? Or do you feel you spend too many of your billable hours talking with prospective patients who never schedule a procedure? Or maybe you're not getting nearly the number of consults that you'd like. If you are looking to increase your monthly billables and grow your practice, then it may be time to rethink your marketing strategy...and your online efforts in particular.

I'm asking because I know that your competition is fierce. While the industry continues to enjoy a healthy 5 percent average annual growth rate, compensation has not kept pace with other fields of medicine. In a 2013 report for the National Center for Policy Analysis, economist Devon Herrick reviewed 20 years of data and found that while medical prices in general have been rising at an average of 5 percent annually, cosmetic surgery prices have moved up only about 1.3 percent a year...not even keeping up with inflation.

And that's not all. While there may be only about 7,000+ licensed plastic surgeons in the United States, you compete with a wide range of *cosmetic surgeons*—physicians in other specialties (e.g., dermatologists, oral surgeons, opthalmologists and otolaryngologists) that perform some subset of plastic procedures. But we're not through. As you well know, the technological advancements that have led to so many new minimally invasive and non-invasive procedures have opened the door to more non-physicians performing cosmetic treatments. So when we factor in all the plastic surgeons, the physicians who can and do call themselves cosmetic surgeons, and the non-physicians we're probably looking at upwards of 60,000 people.

What this means, of course, is that for every Sean McNamara or Robert Rey, there are 100s of qualified plastic surgeons like you trying to build a solid practice in a highly competitive field where the patients who are paying for these elective procedures are actively "shopping" on quality and price in order to receive the greatest value for their out-of-pocket expenditures.

Target Your Best Customers with the Right Message

I wrote this book because despite these issues I see real opportunity for entrepreneurial-minded plastic surgeons willing to invest a couple of hours with me in reading this book. I'm going to show you how the techniques of the most successful businesses in the service sector can help you use the Internet to 1) reach the people most likely to be ready to buy what you have to offer and 2) present your services in such a way as to win the sale and turn prospects into patients.

Now, I'm not equating your medical practice to a car dealership or a plumbing business. I'm not even suggesting you're on par with the local CPA or mortgage business. But increasingly the owners of these types of services are discovering the business boost possible with a smart, aggressive approach to direct marketing. The numbers speak for themselves: According to the Direct Marketing Association (DMA), in the United States direct marketing in all its forms drives annual sales of more than $1.7 trillion. And every year, a larger share of marketing budgets is channeled to Internet direct marketing. With my guidance, you can apply the lessons learned in the service sector to not only grow your practice but actually serve your patients better. That's a real win-win. The approach I'm laying out for you will even cut the non-billable time you spend meeting with prospective patients and answering questions long before they ever schedule an appointment for a surgical procedure or minimally invasive treatment.

...in the United States direct marketing in all its forms drives annual sales of more than $1.7 trillion.

In the pages that follow, I'll introduce you to a marketing technique called **Emotional Direct Response**. This is NOT an Internet get-rich-quick scam either. Direct response is a time-tested marketing technique that works extraordinarily well in the Internet environment. I can honestly tell you that I've used Emotional Direct Response in my own businesses for the past 10 years. The success I've enjoyed and the shear logic of the process has compelled me to want to share my experience and expertise with others. And since moving to Florida more than four years ago, I've seen the proliferation of plastic surgeons in the Miami area—the plastic surgery capital of the world. I believe I have something to say to plastic surgeons like you. Something that will help you rethink how you present your business online, stand out in a crowded field and gain new patients eager for your expertise.

What is Direct Response Marketing?

Direct response is a classic approach for acquiring sales through marketing. It's perhaps the single best tool for growing a successful business or practice today. GEICO, Priceline, LL Bean, Mary Kay Cosmetics and Sears are just a few of the many businesses that use direct response to their advantage. What does direct response look like? It's the catalogs, telemarketing,

con't

---

postcards, infomercials, magazine subscriptions, webinars, and face-to-face sales encounters (to name a few) that you experience every day.

We're going to focus on a highly automated subset of direct response that runs on the Internet. So once your campaign is built, it will deliver prospective patients without a lot of additional effort on your part or that of your marketing partner. It's almost like putting your marketing on autopilot.

Internet-based Emotional Direct Response campaigns bring several additional advantages: *First, they are extremely cost effective* since they eliminate the need for printing and postage. *Second, prospects are highly targeted* due to all the demographic information and viewing habits tracked online. For that matter, through their specific search requests on sites like Google, Bing and Yahoo!, prospective customers effectively self-select and target themselves as people who want what you have to sell. And *third, the many analytical tools available online* help marketers measure their results virtually in real time and, as needed, refine their campaigns to improve results.

No matter what form a direct response campaign takes, all focus on one thing: the bottom line. Now that's key because to be successful, every direct response campaign must deliver a profit...a return on investment (ROI). For every $1 invested, a marketer expects a return of more than $1. Your ROI will depend on a variety of factors (e.g., location, keywords, ad targeting, website) but in a plastic surgery practice—where the lifetime value of a patient runs into the thousands of dollars—the return may be as high as 20:1. By comparison, other, more traditional marketing and advertising techniques are inefficient and less cost effective.

Direct Response—A Formula for Success

The strategy behind Emotional Direct Response Marketing is straightforward and can be broken down into a simple three-step formula:

Website + Direct Response Copy + Traffic

It sounds simple, and on the surface it is. With a minimum of explanation, you can understand the basic strategy and, I think, see a way to better direct your message and market your practice to those most likely to want your services. But marketing programs are a combination of both strategy and tactics. The three-step formula of website, copy and traffic is the strategy; the tactics are all the many little steps and special skills needed to create a successful campaign. But while it's easy enough for a seasoned direct response marketer, I don't expect you to become an expert.

> The strategy behind Emotional Direct Response Marketing is straightforward and can be broken down into a simple three-step formula: Website + Direct Response Copy + Traffic.

Even if you are the managing partner of a large practice and tasked with its continued growth, you should use this book primarily to understand the strategy and why you should use it. Also, as your Emotional Direct Response Marketing campaign comes together, you will need to make several important decisions. This book can help you. But I recommend leaving most of the tactical decisions and their execution to direct response-marketing professionals. If you have an in-house marketer, by all means pass this book along when you finish reading, but again don't expect your marketing specialist to become an overnight expert who's able to affect a perfect Emotional Direct Response campaign—a reality you'll appreciate as this book unfolds.

Why Direct Response Works

Don't confuse direct response with institutional branding or image adverting. Direct response is not about gimmicks, cute mascots, characters or overly cleaver copy. The Goodyear blimp, the GEICO gecko, Keebler elves, Super Bowl ads and most full-color, full-page (i.e., flashy, expensive) print ads in magazines are examples of image advertising. Big companies with deep pockets run these campaigns to keep their names in front of the public with the HOPE that the next time they shop for tires or insurance, cookies or beer or whatever they'll remember the brands and buy their products. That's not bottom-line driven; it's not highly targeted; and most definitely it's not what I'm talking about in this book.

Direct response works because businesses are able to target their prospective clients—people who identify themselves as being interested in buying exactly the solutions you are selling. Emotional Direct Response copy speaks to them in a language and tone that 1) connects, 2) answers many of their most burning questions and 3) leads them directly into the offer with an immediate Call to Action—such as a phone number, link or order form.

Where image advertising focuses on the

con't

---

message a *business* wants to share with the marketplace, direct response is about delivering what *prospects* want to know. That simple distinction means your patients receive the information they need to make a strong commitment to you. Rather than telling and selling, you can bring clarity to the buying decision. As Flint McGlaughlin, director of independent market research lab MECLABS, says, "Clarity trumps persuasion."

Because I know your time is valuable, I've chosen to use Chapter 1 to lay out a hypothetical campaign that will show you how Emotional Direct Response works (and why). The rest of the book breaks down the process step by step and explains the secondary strategies, outlines the tactics, and includes examples for you to consider as you go forward. As I said, I really don't expect you to become a direct marketing expert. The time and money required to develop all the expertise you need is better invested in your profession...what you're trained to do.

At the same time, I realize that a small number of you may become so intrigued by what I'm going to show that you will decide to build your own direct response marketing campaigns. If this is the case, you've started at the right place because I'm going to give you a roadmap for online success. I still recommend, however, that at a minimum you hire a qualified direct response strategic consultant—a Sherpa of sorts to help you navigate the ins and outs and details of your first few efforts. Doing this will get you to the results you want *faster* and with fewer problems and false starts. A good Emotional Direct Response campaign

> ... hire a qualified direct response strategic consultant—a Sherpa of sorts to help you navigate the ins and outs and details of your first few efforts. Doing this will get you to the results you want *faster* and with fewer problems and false starts.

requires the expertise of AdWords professionals, experienced analysts who know how to track ad campaigns, highly qualified copywriters who understand the Emotional Direct Response style, email writers who can set up your follow-up autoresponders and more. Therefore, my best advice: Call me, and together we can discuss how you can BEST put Emotional Direct Response Marketing to work for your practice.

But I'm getting ahead of myself. Before I move into Chapter 1 and begin to explain how Emotional Direct Response works, I'd like to engage you in a quick experiment...one that will give you a little insight into how Emotional Direct Response differs from most Internet marketing efforts. This is the first step toward helping you change forever the way you think about—and use—the Internet.

An Advertising Form That Physicians Can Embrace

In the previous paragraph, I threw out the terms "AdWords" and "ad campaigns." Yes, an Emotional Direct Response campaign uses advertising to drive traffic to your website. And I realize that while completely

con't

---

legal, many physicians are still uncomfortable with advertising. So let me dispel any concerns you might have.

While AdWords *is* a form of advertising, it has very little in common with traditional ad campaigns. AdWords is the Google form for what we call Paid Search or Pay Per Click. I'll go into greater detail about this in the traffic section of this book, but you are already very familiar with Paid Search. It's the small text-based ads that you see every time you run a Google, Bing or other Internet search. The ads are usually positioned on the screen above and to the right of the organic (unpaid) search results that you see.

Just like organic search results, Paid Search uses keywords and keyword phrases to direct people to websites that best match their search criteria. For reasons you'll see, Paid Search does a much better job than pure SEO…reasons that will have a direct impact on your bottom line. "Search," says John Battelle (founder of Federated Media Publishing), "a marketing method that didn't exist a decade ago, provides the most efficient and inexpensive way for businesses to find leads."

Think of AdWords as a hybrid form of advertising in that while your text ads are paid promotions, they are shown *only* to people who are actively searching the topic. You might even say that the people who see your ads have tacitly given permission to you to share your information. And by including the right kind of content on your website, you won't disappoint them.

Oh and by the way, you really do want to reach out to people during the search process. According to the results of a recent study by PR giant Fleishman-Hillard International Communications and Harris

con't

Interactive, fully 89 percent of consumers report that they turn to Search to find information about services, products and businesses…before they buy. You need to be there.

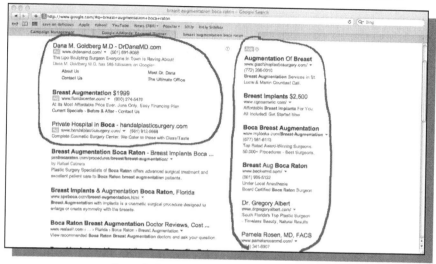

I've circled the Paid Search Ads above

What Can You Expect from a Typical Website?

To begin, if your practice has a website, turn to your computer and open your site in a browser window right now. And while you're at it, open the websites of four or five other plastic surgeons you know. Or just for fun, Google plastic surgeons in any city in the country and select a few websites. It really doesn't matter because I can practically guarantee that every website you look at is going to be pretty much the same. Oh the colors and photos will be different. As will the basic formats, templates, even the number of pages. But here's what you're going to see:

- You'll come first to a homepage with the photo of one or more attractive people. There might also be a photo of the surgeon or surgical team.

- The headline announces the doctor's name, or the name of the surgery center. If particularly effusive, the headline might even invite prospective patients to "call for a free consultation today for beautiful results tomorrow." Or some such line.

- Under the headline, the body copy briefly extols the medical team's years of experience and its many satisfied patients. It reassures prospective patients that the physicians have an excellent reputation and the practice is trusted in the community.

- And now I'm going to bet that between the homepage copy and all the pages that collectively make up the website, the physicians have made sure to list every treatment they're prepared to do—from breast augmentations and facelifts to tummy tucks and liposuction. Plus all the injections, peels, laser and abrasion treatments. The typical plastic surgery website is a veritable smorgasbord of procedures.

- But we're just getting warmed up. On the more elaborate and expensive sites, there may be anywhere from eight to 10 pages plus a blog. The homepage may include links to the practice on Facebook, Twitter and other social media. (I'll talk more about that when we get into the Traffic section of the book.) And more than likely, there is a page each for breast, body, face and skin treatments available.

- Now to every practice that includes both "before and after" pictures and testimonials from happy patients, I congratulate the physicians. These are definitely things that visitors want to see. **There's just one problem:** The examples have probably been selected to remind visitors yet again that theirs is a full-service practice and surgical center able to do a wide range of cosmetic procedures.

19

I'm pretty sure I've described what you're seeing to a T because I've looked at enough sites to know that this is a safe bet. I'll also bet that right about now you're scratching your head and saying, "So what, Marc? A lot of those sites look very nice. I was even envious of one or two."

I'll even agree with you. Many of the sites are terrific to look at. Nice graphics, good typography, and a clean layout. And yes, they even say a lot about what the practice does...maybe too much. The problem is they're digital brochures and no more effective than brand or image advertising. Sites like these rarely lead to more appointments or consultations. And please understand that in pointing this out, I'm not criticizing you or slamming other plastic surgeons.

The truth is most industries and professions approach the web in the same way. According to search software provider WordStream, its review in 2013 of 500 small and medium businesses running AdWords Pay Per Click campaigns showed that 20 percent are hurting their chances of converting traffic into customers and patients by directing interested prospects to generic brochure sites. To make sure you don't make this same mistake, I'll show you how to optimize your site for the best results.

Only someone who fully understands Emotional Direct Response Marketing will have a website that is able to reach out and grab the attention of prospective patients and speak to their *specific* wants and needs. Only the *best* Emotional Direct Response campaigns use a carefully designed website to get highly motivated prospects to take the next step.

Only the *best* Emotional Direct
Response campaigns use a carefully
designed website to get highly
motivated prospects to take
the next step.

All the websites you just looked at—even the best-looking ones—are digital brochures that include a little something for everyone, a whole lot about the physician(s) and the practice, and not much designed to convince prospective patients that this is the plastic surgeon best able to perform precisely the procedure they want—which is what people need to make an emotional connection and, ultimately, an educated buying decision. Brochure sites are not written with patients' needs in mind. They don't speak to their concerns, fears, questions and self-esteem issues. Nor do they focus the message on one particular treatment or procedure. And that, as you're about to discover, is a big mistake. Brochure sites are more like digital tours of the facilities and the people who work there...with a few happy customer testimonials and before-and-after pictures thrown in as proof of results.

So do I have your attention? Are you ready to know more about how you can use the Internet to reach highly targeted prospective patients and pre-sell them so effectively they can't wait to take the next step? Are you ready to learn how an Emotional Direct Response Marketing program can help you build your practice?

Then let's get started.

Chapter 1
Epic Fail!
Mega-Website Mistakes!

"The first thing you need to know is that your current website is failing you!"

–Marc Savage

I f this was a straight how-to book, I'd simply lay out step by step and decision by decision how to launch an Emotional Direct Response campaign. But because I believe you should be working with marketing experts who can run your campaign—all or in part—I don't think that's the best way to get you started. Rather, I'm going to take you through a hypothetical campaign and show you HOW Emotional Direct Response differs from what probably 98 percent of businesses with websites are doing today.

First, let's do a little reality check, and you can admit it. I left you in a bit of a quandary at the end of the Introduction by pointing out the digital-brochure approach you can expect to see on most sites and suggesting that it isn't the best strategy. Worse than that: It's why most websites fail. And by fail, I mean why the typical brochure site doesn't deliver prospective patients ready to schedule appointments with you.

The short answer to why they fail is this: You have roughly 3 seconds to make your first impression and connect with visitors to your website before they backclick and choose another website to visit.

The short answer to why they fail is this: You have roughly 3 seconds to make your first impression and connect with visitors to your website before they backclick and choose another website to visit. If you don't speak to them (make a strong connection) in those 3 seconds, they're gone, and your website has failed to market your expertise to a prospective patient.

The failure comes from trying to be everything to everyone and not making any individual feel that you are an expert in the procedure he or she wants AND that you understand exactly why they feel the need for cosmetic surgery. Remember, you are on the Internet to find clients for your services—prospective patients who want the cosmetic procedures and treatments you offer. But when you spend money building your website, having copy written and hosting that website on the Internet, and then don't make money...that's a fail. Low return on investment (ROI) is the fail.

Now one caveat: As a plastic surgeon, if you get a couple of people who call you from a website that you spent $10,000 to develop—and you get one breast augmentation and one facelift a year from that—your website has paid for itself and even made a profit because you're making anywhere from $5,000 to $10,000 per surgical procedure. Technically you made money on your website. But rather than getting one breast augmentation, one facelift and maybe a liposuction, what if you can get 20 breast augmentations? A month? How does that sound? That's the potential I'm talking about with a professionally crafted Emotional Direct Response Marketing campaign that is fully optimized for success.

And I'm going to go out on a limb here, but if you're like most business owners, you probably don't even know whether or not your website is making money because you're not tracking the metrics. You're not using the panoply of online analytical tools (many free) available to help you know exactly what your website is doing. This is going to be even more important as you begin to advertise online. Without information on the number of ad impressions and click throughs to your website (on Pay Per Click)...without a good general sense of traffic...and without knowing how many website visitors actually contact your office and, ultimately become patients (we call that conversion)...without all that, you can't say that for every dollar you spend on your website marketing that you're getting even a dollar in ROI—let alone a dollar plus.

Again, I'm not being critical. You're a doctor. You didn't study marketing and probably don't spend a lot of time researching marketing strategies now that you're managing your practice. Nor should you. But someone must.

The reason I know your situation is because I was like you—before I learned what direct response marketing was all about. Let me share a little personal story, and maybe this will sound familiar to you:

When I had my mortgage business, I started my first advertising in the Yellow Pages. A rep came to my office and said, "Hey, you ought to be in the Yellow Pages if you own a business." Well, that made sense to me. I too had to have an ad in the Yellow Pages. I also assumed, like most people, that the bigger the ad, the better. Of course, the sales rep agreed. "The bigger the ad, the better because you want to stand out from your competition," he said. "What's more, if you add colors, you'll stand out even more than ones that don't have multiple colors. Bigger type, more color, eye-grabbing graphics—that's what you need." Not better, just more because more is better. In truth, more just costs more money. It certainly didn't give me better results. I didn't get one single phone call from my ad. Well, maybe I got one, but I can't really say because, like you, I just did what I thought I was supposed to do, and I didn't measure the results. I just *assumed* I was on the right track because that's what everyone else did.

But it's *incestuous marketing*, built on generations of bad assumptions and herd mentality. You know what happens when people have incest. The same thing happens with your marketing results when you copy and perpetuate the mistakes of the majority. We all go out and look in the Yellow Pages and see what everybody else is doing. Then we copy it. And we assume that because they're doing it (and they've been doing it for longer than we have) that it works. The truth is they probably copied from somebody else. And so on. The reps reinforce this behavior and even tell you to look at what others in your field are doing. "Just kind of copy it," they say, "only make yours stand out more." But it doesn't work in the Yellow Pages, and it most definitely doesn't work with website design and copywriting.

25

> But it's *incestuous marketing*, built on generations of bad assumptions and herd mentality.

Sooner or later you find out the hard way that you're not getting any business from your marketing effort. Maybe you just start asking people how they found you; that's a simple form of tracking. One way or another, eventually you discover what a waste of resources you marketing effort has been. Because you don't know how to fix the problem, you take the next most logical action and simply stop advertising in the Yellow Pages altogether—and effectively stop marketing. With my help, you're about to turn all that around and not make the same mistake on the Internet.

In telling you this story, I'm not slamming the Yellow Pages although the truth is these days most people are turning to the Internet. They're running local searches to find what they need, and that only ups the ante for you, making it all the more important for you to take the right approach with your website. But plumbers, electricians, and all those people you need to call in an emergency can still use the printed Yellow Pages effectively if they take the time to be strategic about their marketing and advertising. We all need to understand what will make us stand out in the marketplace and catch the eye, the interest, of our potential customers and give them a reason to call us *versus* somebody else.

Why Having A Strategy Matters: Play Along at Home

Before we move into completely into digital promotion, let's take apart some Yellow Pages ads. I want you to see just how prevalent incestuous marketing really is and how muddled most messaging becomes because of it. The Yellow Pages are built on pure competition. No one just browses. People using the Yellow Pages are looking for solutions and usually immediate solutions. Advertisers are competing with other, similar service providers in their community. They should be trying to best the competition with strategic messages that reach out and grab the prospective customer emotionally by anticipating what prospects are looking for then driving home the benefits. But as you'll see, the headlines and ad copy is all remarkably similar and the primary differences are in size and color.

You can play along at home; just pick a service category in your Yellow Pages, and you'll see exactly the same kinds of problems as the ones I'll be pointing out. I live in south Florida; it's 80 degrees most of the time. If my air conditioning breaks down at any time of the year, I'm not happy. If I have an air conditioning problem, I need it fixed...fast. So I'm breaking open the Yellow Pages and turning to the air conditioning repair section. I'm not going to name names; I don't want to embarrass anyone. But you'll get the point.

The first ad I see is a two-page ad, and the headline reads, "24-Hour Emergency Same-Day Service." That gets my attention because I need that...now. The second thing it says is "Free Estimates or Free Second Opinion." Well, that's good, I guess. But then I read, "Call now for a free estimate." And I'm reminded that I'm hot and have no time for second options or estimates. Not a lot of thought went into considering what the customer who needs 24-hour service really requires. This company has lost me. I won't be picking up the phone because I have the phone book and plenty of other air conditioning companies I can choose. Yes, I have an emergency. Yes, I want this fixed ASAP. But how long does it take me to flip from one page to the next?

So now my eye falls on another big ad, and I see that this company is the Number One Rheem Team contractor in the nation. But I don't have a Rheem. I'm not actually sure what I have, but I don't think it's a Rheem. They may service other brands, but by specifying Rheem they've discouraged me from calling when they might have been able to fix my problem. This is a bad example of targeting a niche market (something we're going to explore in depth), and they just lost me as a customer. Next.

I see another two-page ad with almost the same basic headline as in the first one. And it's a smart headline: "24/7-Hour Emergency Service." They're 24/7, which is actually better than the other guys who were just 24-hour. This is seven days a week. I'm not saying it's a better headline. In fact, it's terrible because it's practically the same as the other company, but at least it speaks to one of the requirements of a person who need immediate service. The ad also says "We sell and service all makes and models." Good, at least they have me covered. This is a possibility, but I'm not convinced this is my best choice. I'm going to keep looking.

Right underneath is another 24/7 ad with virtually the exact same headline. Are you seeing a pattern? No original thinking here. And under the headline, it reads, "A company you can trust." That's nice, but I would hope I could trust them. You have to wonder who the competition is when someone has to say that. A company I can't trust? It doesn't do anything for me, but at least it didn't chase me away. There's a picture of their trucks with the caption: "Sales, service, installation. All makes and models. Complete A/C maintenance. Air purification. 100 percent financing." But so far they haven't said in any uncertain words that they're going to fix my problem. Meanwhile, I'm sweating my brains out. I'm not picking up the phone to call.

Next headline: "Air conditioning broken?" Ooh, I like that. Yes, it is. This is also a two-page ad, and it says, "All work guaranteed." I like that too. They've included a list of all the different air conditioning brands they service. Clearly they're

28

pros. I'm interested. More copy: "There's a better way to keep cool. Service you can trust. All makes and models. Free second opinions. Sales, service, installation." This is better, but it's still not making me call. They haven't hit my button. Yes, my air conditioning is broken, but they haven't said they're going to come right over and fix it. That's assumed, but you never leave an assumption up to the consumer. They could have said: "Air conditioning broken? We'll fix it or it's free." That's a headline that would have had my attention. I'd be picking up the phone and calling. Instead, I'm moving on.

This is the most typical of all, and I've changed the name and date to hide their identity. Here's the headline: "Air City, LLC. Family-owned and operated since 1985. Our business is your family's comfort. BBB accredited. A+ rating." But they're not finished patting themselves on the back yet. The ad continues: "Same-day air conditioning, heating and service. Licensed and insured." That's better than the name of the company, but not much. They're proud of their credentials, but are they going to fix my broken air conditioner?

Below that, the next headline reads: "Residential, commercial, industrial. Sales and service. All makes and models." In smaller type, the ad says: "24-hour emergency service." And then they've included a big, huge phone number. The only reason I might call them is because I've gone through six others. At this point, they all look pretty much the same. I'm hot, so I'm just going to pick one at random now. It might be this one. It might not. Who knows?

Create a Strategy That Works: Three Key Lessons

By now, you should be scared of incestuous marketing and have a good understanding of what doesn't work. Let's now focus on the essential elements you'll need to build a successful strategy. I've broken them into three critical lessons.

LESSON ONE—FOCUS ON A NICHE: Even though you perform many cosmetic procedures and treatments, your direct response website must focus on ONE specific procedure. Don't try to promote general medicine or even plastic surgery.

So let's say that in addition to facelifts and rhinoplasties, chemical peels and Botox treatments, you do several augmentation mammaplasties each month. And let's also say that while you perform a wide range of procedures, you particularly like doing breast augmentations. It's a relatively simple surgery, completed on average in about 2 ½ hours. And when the patient is a good candidate for the procedure (with her expectations reasonably set) she's going to leave your care a very happy individual. In addition, at between $5,000 and $10,000 the remuneration is excellent. And since this is one of the most popular cosmetic surgical procedures today, the field of potential patients is big.

So let me ask you this: If you want patients who want breast augmentations to come to you, why would you send them to a website that talks about liposuction and facelifts and hair transplants and includes breast augmentation as just one among the many procedures you perform? Think of it this way. On a generic brochure site, you're saying, I do everything. I do facelifts; let me tell you a little bit about facelifts. I do breast augmentations; let me tell you a little bit about breast augmentations. And so on. You only have space for a few little paragraphs. If you're lucky, it's three paragraphs on the website about each procedure. You cannot expect people to spend out of pocket for an elective procedure and allow you to cut them open based on a few paragraphs. That's not how you get somebody to call you.

> You cannot expect people to spend out of pocket for an elective procedure and allow you to cut them open based on a few paragraphs.

Take Sarah; she's one of our hypothetical patients. For Sarah to come in and meet with you takes effort and time out of her day. She's asking herself, *Why should I come in? You're a licensed plastic surgeon. Well, so is every other plastic surgeon. Why you? What do you do that the others can't do just as well? I just happened to land on your site, and finally after reviewing 14 other sites I'm ready and I just happened to be on your site when I was ready to pick up the phone and call.* It's great that you were in the right place at the right time when her resistence was finally exhausted—just as mine did after looking at several ads for air conditioning repair. The problem is Sarah could have just as easily been on another physician's website when she made her decision to call. You need to me more strategic if Sarah, or any prospect, is going to stick on your site and not feel the need to move on. In addition, that generic "something for everyone" website will leave her with a lot of unanswered questions. You still have a lot of work to do before she agrees to schedule a procedure with you...and you could still lose her business along the way.

And another thing, let's say that Sarah does find your website and decides to arrange for a free consultation to come in and discuss the possibility of a procedure. You've now had to set aside time in your schedule. Oh, and by the way, Sarah has made similar appointments with two or three of your colleagues in town. She may even meet with one of the others first, be wildly impressed (after all, you're all good at what you do) and never show at your office. You've just wasted valuable time in your busy day on a no-show. To quote David Siteman Garland, host of the Internet TV show *The Rise to the Top*: "Money follows passion and not the other way around." There's not much passion in a generic brochure site.

To succeed, you need a dedicated website that talks only about breast augmentation—if that's what you choose to promote. The instant Sarah lands on your site, you want her to know that you are speaking to her...that you care as much about her breast augmentation as she does. You want her to find answers to her most urgent questions. Your goal is for Sarah to see you as THE expert in town in this particular procedure so she takes the next step and contacts your office. You want that call—from Sarah or anyone—to come from a person who is in a sense pre-sold on you just from having read your website. A website that actually CONVERTS interested (highly targeted) visitors by encouraging them to take action...now that's a successful website!

An all-inclusive brochure site will not make you money. This is true across virtually all businesses in the service sector, and it's the same in your profession. Every plastic surgeon offers the same range of cosmetic procedures and treatments. There are some exceptions, particularly when it comes to reconstructive surgery, but by and large you're all offering the same thing. And assuming a certain level of competency, one facelift is more or less the same as another facelift. One breast augmentation is the same as another. Different pictures. Different colors. But it's basically all the same...nothing to make you stand out from the pack. There's certainly nothing to make a prospective patient pick you over one of your colleagues.

So now if you go back and look at some of the same websites you looked at earlier—even the ones that you thought were great—you'll begin to see how much everybody's website looks like...well, incestuous marketing. And yes, they all do facelifts. They all inject Botox and fillers. They all do breast augmentations. Where's the focus? Where's the specialization? Where's the sense of expertise that a prospective patient is looking for?

Your strategic objective is to differentiate yourself by focusing your website on one procedure—what we call a niche. A niche website is optimized by specializing in exactly the procedure a targeted prospect is looking for. And by narrowing your focus to one procedure, you can expand on the subject and answer Sarah's questions in greater depth. And you can bet that you'll stand out as the real expert in the field.

LESSON TWO—SPEAK YOUR PATIENTS' LANGUAGE: While it may be important to tell a prospective patient about yourself, that's not the message that will make the first connection. Before people think logically, they react emotionally.

The other big thing, and this is huge, is most websites are about the wrong person. Most websites are all about you the doctor (or in the case of service companies, you the businessperson). But every prospective patient or client on the planet is tuned into the exact same radio station. We all are tuned into WIIFM—What's In It For Me?

"Well," you say, "patients only have to read my site to know I'm good. I've had excellent training, expertise in breast augmentation, years of experience, top credentials, and I'm respected both in the community and among my peers. That's why I put all that information on the front page of my website."

That's great. But nobody's reading your site. Remember, you have 3 seconds to get somebody's attention. In those 3 seconds, you have to make a powerful connection just to have a chance of being read. And your fabulous credentials just won't do it.

The real truth is, Sarah doesn't care about you. Another of our hypothetical patients, Tom, who's looking for a hair transplant, doesn't care about you either. None of them care about you or what you do. Now, of course, they do, but before they care about who you are and what you do and how you do it, they want to know, what's in it for me?

> ...before they care about who you are and what you do and how you do it, they want to know, What's in it for me?

Sarah's looking for a breast augmentation, and in all likelihood her self-esteem is low. It doesn't matter whether it's justified or not. She's on your website and considering surgery, going through a painful procedure, and allowing you to put something in her chest to make her breasts larger because her self-esteem is low. She may be looking forward to the results, but the procedure is not fun. Her personal issues are foremost in her mind—along with her questions and maybe even a few concerns.

Coming to a website that says you're a plastic surgeon and a respected member of the community doesn't tell her anything about the real things going on in her head. Unless your message jumps out at her immediately and speaks to her issues, she's gone. She's going somewhere else to find somebody whose message does jump out and speak to her.

Making the homepage all about you and your abilities is more of the same old incestuous-marketing myth. Like you, physicians all know that ability and experience are important. Thus, because everyone else leads with this information, you should to. Wrong! Because it's not the first thing that Sarah and the thousands of other women considering breast augmentation need to *feel* about you before they can think about your skills.

You've probably heard the saying, content is king. But what kind of content should you use? I find it's interesting that the majority of top companies surveyed say they are adding more and better content to their websites. This decision coincides with the results of a 2013 Digital Advertising Alliance Poll that found that more than 90 percent of Americans say that free content is important to the value of the Internet. I caution that your message needs to be strategically determined. In other words, if your content is going to educate people and help them ultimately make a buying decision, your message first needs to speak to their emotional needs. This is the key is to moving people to pick up the phone and call.

To do this right, you need a web presence that grabs the prospective patient emotionally in those critical 3 seconds. You need a web presence that speaks to Sarah's desire to be the envy of every woman on the beach, or to Tom's dream of women wanting to run their fingers through his gorgeous mop of hair. And this is not just true for the Web. This applies to any marketing you're doing. Whatever media you choose for your direct response, your message must speak to the emotional issues first. You can't be logical or clinical. You have to be human...and know what resonates with the kinds of people who seek cosmetic surgery.

What Is *Emotional* Direct Response?

We've learned a lot in recent years about how the brain works. One of the things we know is that our messages, when received in the brain, do not automatically reach the neocortex—the most advanced and logical part of our brain. Not at first. It's our "lizard" brain that serves as a gatekeeper, of sorts, to the rest of the brain's functions. In other words, if your message doesn't satisfy the lizard brain, the rest of the brain doesn't even have a chance of getting your message.

To satisfy the lizard brain, your message must be simple, fresh, provocative and nonthreatening. This is the message that has to get through in those critical first 3 seconds. If your message passes the lizard test, it has a chance of resonating with the middle brain, or limbic—where emotional messages are processed—and only then the neocortex.

So what does this mean to your marketing? Well, simply that the first thing a person hears or reads is going to determine if your facts and figures ever get a chance to be considered by our higher-order thinking. With the lizard brain and limbic satisfied, the neocortex can take complex information and make sense of it and turn it into actionable decisions. All your facts and figures are wasted if they don't reach the neocortex.

An Emotional Direct Response copywriter can help you craft a message that breaks through the 3-second barrier, intrigues the lizard brain, evokes emotion in the limbic and makes your logical case to the neocortex.

So what if you had a headline on your website about breast augmentation, and the first thing that Sarah saw was, "Be the Envy of Every Woman on the Beach this Summer." Or, "Would You Like to Fill Out Any Bathing Suit or Top You Want to Wear?" These may not be great headlines, but you get the point. They're about Sarah and her issues. There's nothing about you the doctor…not yet. And now she's interested. Now she might be intrigued enough to peruse your site and stick around long enough to learn something about you. If your headline speaks to prospective patients, chances are they'll remain on your site longer than 3 seconds.

The same thing is true with Tom. When he shows up at your site all about hair transplantation and immediately reads a headline that says: "Does Thinning Hair Make You Feel Old Beyond Your Years?" Or, "Does Remembering the 'Good Old Days' Make You Wish for a Thick Head of Hair?" You're message is probably going to begin to resonate. Tom is thinking…that's me. That's what I'm looking for.

I've simplified the process to make my point, which is: Only after you've addressed Tom's or Sarah's or any individual's needs will they pay attention to the rest of your message. When Tom feels receptive and Sarah feels comfortable and everyone in your target audience is emotionally invested in your message, that's the time to talk about yourself. And the place for that will be your About Us page. That's where you tell readers that you're a licensed plastic surgeon who has done 8 million breast implants in the last 20 years.

You Emotional Direct Response website is comprised of just five pages. It should be built on the WordPress platform as it's one of the easiest and least expensive ways to build a site, and the process of updating and making text changes is easy enough that most people in your office should be up to the task of making minor changes and regularly adding new before-and-after photos and more happy-patient testimonials. Your website should be laid out in this order:

- **The Main or Homepage:** We often call this the Landing Page since it is the page people will typically land on first when they come to your site. It's the page your AdWords Pay Per Click ad drives them to first, which is why this is the page that has to make the emotional connection. It's the critical page. Do it right, and people might just stay around to see the rest.

  The copy is in the style of a long-form sales letter, which is a copywriting term for the text that makes your case. It's like the multi-page sales letters you receive in the mail from a credit card company or an auto insurance agency that grab your attention with an emotionally charged headline and then go on to explain exactly why you need what they are selling. The only difference is that instead of a printed letter, yours is displayed on the website. It can be as long as you need it to be to make your argument, deliver on the promise in your headline and make your offer. And no longer. It's not about padding out the homepage; it's about making the very best emotional case you (with the help of your copywriter) can make. The other four pages are your supporting evidence.

- **About Us:** This is where you tell *your* story. You can talk about your training, your education, the number of years you've been practicing and the certifications and other credentials you hold. The focus is on the people (you and other doctors in the practice). Remember, people do business with other people...not companies...or practices...or surgical centers.

- **FAQ Page:** FAQ stands for Frequently Asked Questions. You use this page to anticipate what prospective patients most want to know. It's part of your initial effort to inform and resolve some of their issues and concerns. Ideally, you'll answer their most emotional issues in the long-form sales letter on the homepage. But in time as you and your staff find yourselves repeatedly answering the same questions by phone or during a consultation, you'll get a good sense of some of the questions that can easily be answered here. This is not a comprehensive list, just a few of the most commonly asked questions that can help to further set expectations.

- **Before and After Page:** While everyone is interested in results, in plastic surgery it's all about how people are going to look after your procedure. Will their wrinkles disappear? Will their lips be full but not too extreme? Will their breasts be perky and beautiful? And their hair transplants look natural? They want to envision themselves in the "after" pictures and be reassured that you have the skill to give them the look they want. As the saying goes, a picture is worth 1000 words.

- **Testimonial Page:** Here's where you let your happy patients speak on your behalf. Actually, you're not going to call this a testimonial page. Once again you're going to play to the emotions and expectations of prospective patients and call this something like: The Natural Hair Page, The Mommies with Tight Tummies Page, The Looking Younger Page, The Beautiful Breasts Page, The Satisfied Patients Page. You get the point, and a top-notch copywriter can work with you to come up with just the right adjectives or metaphors to generate the emotional reaction you want. The name you pick will reinforce the niche you've chosen to target, and it's one more reminder that you do beautiful work.

- **Call to Action:** I slipped this in here. It's not really a sixth page on your website, but it is critical. With your website built, and your emotional copy speaking directly to each visitor, building a strong connection, acknowledging their wants and desires, and making each visitor feel that you are the right—*the only*—choice, your site needs one more component: A strong Call to Action. You need to tell people how to take the next step. In other words, once you've demonstrated your good bedside manner, made it easy for them to make a commitment...even if it's just to watch a special video you've created or download a free report that goes into greater depth on the procedure and outcomes. I'll be talking a lot about this in later chapters, but here I'll just speak to the obvious. To win the business, you need visitors to take the next logical step. If you want them to pick up the phone and speak to someone in your office or book a free consultation, you need to make this your Call to Action. Give them your phone number, tell them to download your free report or give them a way to link to your video. And put your offer on each of your five pages. Without people taking action, you have a nice site that doesn't make it easy for prospects to take the next step to becoming your patient.

To be strategic, you must remember that initial decisions are always emotional. Logic only enables people to justify their emotional decisions—to themselves and to their friends and family. Optimize your website for success by connecting with prospective patients emotionally. Follow this with your credentials. And be sure to make your Call to Action appealing.

LESSON THREE—MAKE PAID SEARCH YOUR FIRST STRATEGY: While blogging, social media and organic search through search engine optimization (SEO) are popular ways to build traffic and find prospects, the time and challenges a marketer faces to get results are onerous. Plus, the conversion rate for turning social and organic prospects into clients is extremely low.

Now that you have a website and copy optimized to convert, you're ready to start bringing as many highly targeted people as possible to your new website. While there are many ways to promote your website—through social media posting, blogging, search engine optimization (SEO), and social media advertising—we're going to focus on Paid Search advertising. These are the brief, text-based, AdWords ads that will catch the attention of someone searching on what you have to offer.

When our Sarah searches something like "Best Breast Augmentation Surgeon Miami" (or whatever city), it's your Pay Per Click ad that needs to come up on page one of the search results. You want the same for Tom. When he enters "Boca Raton Plastic Surgeon for Hair Transplant," it's your ad that needs to be at the top of the first page of search results.

Paid Search is the fastest—most optimal—way to get the results you want, and I'll explain why in detail in Chapter 4. At this time, I'll only say that the hours spent blogging and building a base of friends and followers on Facebook or Twitter is not time well spent...at least not initially. Furthermore, studies show that conversion rates for social are lower than Paid Search leads—in all likelihood because the people who are simply interested in subject are not necessarily as ready to move forward as those who are searching for a plastic surgeon in their area to perform a specific procedure or treatment.

It stands to reason that someone who enters a search for "Find Breast Augmentation Surgeon Miami" is more interested in buying than the person who decides to follow you on Facebook. Social media, SEO, even blogging all have their place, but these are long-term strategies that won't deliver the patients you want now. Direct response marketing using AdWords is the only short-term strategy optimized for immediate results. It's your best return on investment.

If you run a search on Google or Bing, you'll notice that the paid ads at the very top of the page and in the right-hand column sort of wrap around the organic search results. They are selected to appear based on the keywords just as the organic results. And Pay Per Click removes many of the impediments of organic Google search, as you'll see. But the key to Paid Search is its ability to reach a highly targeted audience...one that is actively looking for the procedure or treatment you are offering.

You can run ad campaigns on Google, Bing, or any search engine that offers Pay Per Click. But for the examples throughout this book, I'll focus on Google. It's the biggest, most sophisticated and most successful PPC program available. On average, Google receives more than 5 billion search requests a day...that's more than 2 million a minute!

Once you have your PPC campaign in place, you have to watch to see if it works. Are you reaching your best target audience? Are people clicking on your ads? Are they taking advantage of your Call to Action? Are you getting people coming to your office who first saw you on the Internet? Are you starting to do more procedures in the niche you decided to target? While from a technical standpoint, there's more to analysis than this— which is why I recommend working with a professional—answers to these questions are opportunities to further optimize your campaign and improve results.

Once you have a website proven to convert visitors into patients your heavy lifting is done. From here on out, you're measuring its success. You may have to tweak a few things for optimal results. Maybe you'll have to change your headline. Or you may decide that your long-form sales letter needs a few refinements. Perhaps you'll even decide to change the picture on the homepage. And on the traffic side, your AdWords copy may need refining. You may want to buy more keyword phrases or drop others. These are all tweaks...and the truth is you never stop analyzing and tweaking. That's how you keep increasing your ROI.

A strategy for optimal access to highly targeted prospective patients requires that you identify the keyword phrases they are using to search for a plastic surgeon in your area. Working with a traffic expert will help you make the right choices, monitor results and adjust as necessary to continue improving your results. Getting your AdWords message in front of those prospects most likely to click through and ultimately move forward for surgery or a minimally invasive treatment is an ongoing effort. If tracking and testing is showing us nothing else, it's that analysis is a critical component of successful marketing today.

At this point, I've given you the gist of an Emotional Direct Response Marketing campaign using extraordinarily broad brushstrokes. But I think you can begin to see the logic of this approach. It's fast. It's effective. And it works. It's why a 2013 Ascend2 study of business leaders and marketers found that only 8 percent of respondents were either not using Pay Per Click or making plans to use it.

So now, if you're ready to take control of your Internet presence and increase the number of prospective patients coming to you via your website, then let's dive into the details.

Chapter 2
Metrics Before Marketing!
Analyze Your Patients
and Your Practice!

"If it doesn't sell, it isn't creative"

– David Ogilvy

Chapter 1 was our view of the Emotional Direct Response process from 50,000 feet. Now it's time to come back down to earth and work through the many steps involved in setting up a campaign. I've divided this section into two chapters: In Chapter 3, we'll focus on website layout, headlines, copywriting and all the elements that go into site design. For this, you'll want to work with professional site designers and copywriters, and a direct response strategic consultant can help you find the right resources.

But first, in this chapter, we're going to discuss the *essential* business decisions you need to make BEFORE you can create a successful direct response website or advertising

44

campaign. We're going to look into your practice and analyze some of the procedures and treatments you perform—not from a medical perspective but in business terms. The more you know about your business and the lifetime value of a patient—and the outcomes you want from a direct response campaign—the better your decisions. The conclusions you reach in this chapter provide the lynchpin for a successful direct response campaign.

I've said this before, but I can't repeat it enough. The purpose of your direct response website is to make money...NOW. Not in two years. Not even six months. Image advertisers can only hope that if people see their ads dozens of times maybe they will remember the brand when the time eventually comes to shop. But that's not your business model. You don't want people to have to see your Pay Per Click (PPC) ads dozens of times, and you don't want them repeatedly clicking on your ads as each clickthrough costs you money. Nor do you want them to visit your website multiple times on the chance that someday they will say something like, "You know, I'm thinking about having a facelift. I remember there was this website out there...now where did I see that? Oh yes, I think that might have been Dr. Brown's site...or was it Dr. Ruiz? I'm pretty sure it was Dr. Brown; I should call her office today."

> Direct response is about immediacy ...efficiency...and urgency. It's about generating a desire to act and imparting the confidence to move forward with you.

Direct response is about immediacy...efficiency...and urgency. It's about generating a desire to act and imparting the confidence to move forward with you. Without a solid direct response formula (**Website + Emotional Copy + Traffic**) prospective patients will be tentative. And calls from tentative people require too much work on the back end—answering questions, selling your expertise and getting prospects to commit. You want to avoid this as much as possible.

Within minutes (a couple of days at most) of finding your Paid Search ad and clicking through to your website, a prospective patient could be moving forward and scheduling an appointment with you. But this only works when your setup and execution are spot on—or as I've been saying, optimized for results. Making the right decisions now will help ensure that your:

1. Prospects find your ad at precisely the right time in the buying cycle—when actively searching for a plastic surgeon.

2. Message is focused on exactly what prospective patients are looking for when they're ready to purchase—the one (and only one) procedure they want.

3. Prospects perceive you to be the expert in the field—focusing on their needs and concerns and answering their questions elevates you above the rest of the field.

4. Business metrics give insight into what you're selling and why—knowing the lifetime value of a patient and the ROI of each procedure will help you choose the right market niche.

When you do everything right, you should see a significant increase in your close rate (the number of prospects who become patients), while you spend less time in face-to-face consultations "selling" them on your services. It's not about selling and telling or strong-arm tactics. It's about using your website to make a strong emotional connection and to provide targeted information that leads to a prospective patient taking action—in effect pre-selling on autopilot.

So let's examine each of the above conditions and the business decisions you need to make before starting to build your website and your direct response campaign.

Target Active Buyers: Enter Later in the Buying Cycle

One word describes the role of Internet search in our lives today—ubiquitous. We all do it dozens of times every day. But all searches are not equal. Sometimes we are looking for a quick fact or figure or name; other times we are conducting in-depth research on a topic; and sometimes we are seeking the best place to buy a product or service. Search often begins long before we are ready to purchase. And the more expensive the product or service, the more time we are likely to spend in study and deliberation.

In the world of image advertising and branding, the process of reaching a buying decision requires as many as eight to 12 "touches" before a prospect becomes a customer, where a touch is the intersection of brand and prospective buyer. It's the number of times someone needs to see your name, your brand, or your ad before taking action. So at eight to 12 touches, people need to experience some combination of advertising, email, word of mouth, website, social media, store display, telemarketing (and more) 8 to 12 times before they will buy.

There are probably only two types of purchases that happen without a lot of thought and consideration and weighing of options:

1.   The **impulse purchase**--when shoppers pick up a small item at the checkout counter or add something extra to their online shopping cart before checking out. But even this only works

because the customer has already stepped up and committed to buy something, thus passing the biggest hurdle. It's easier to get them to buy just a little bit more. Whatever brought them to the store or website in the first place, they've already been through the decision-making steps and had sufficient touches to commit to the purchase.

2. The **urgent or emergency purchase**—when a water pipe bursts at 10 PM on a Sunday night and the basement is filing with water, we grab the Yellow Pages or jump on the Internet to find any plumber in our community who makes house calls 24/7/365. Urgency takes priority over a long, protracted search or multiple touches. Similarly, if a child falls and cuts his head, we're only worried about the bleeding and the risk of concussion. It's an emergency; we don't spend a lot of time weighing options and interviewing doctors. We want two things: the closest hospital and an expert on staff to attend to the child.

For virtually everything else, the decision-making process can be lengthy. The prospective patient (or customer) needs to be won over and given sufficient reason to buy from you. But you can reduce the time and touches needed to sell someone on your professional services by *deliberately* getting in front of the prospect late in the decision-making cycle— after much of the preliminary information gathering is done...when they are actively looking to buy.

...you can reduce the time and touches needed to sell someone on your professional services by deliberately getting in front of the prospect late in the decision-making cycle...

You can't change how people make decisions or the number of preliminary touches they require to move forward. You can, however, control HOW and WHEN you present yourself. So let people go to generic plastic surgery information sites or talk with friends who have had procedures. Let them seek out advice on social sites or even go to your competitors' brochure sites in the early phases. You don't use Paid Search to educate the merely curious. Only when they are serious about searching for a local plastic surgeon who performs a particular procedure does your ad need to appear in the search results. That's when you want to be able to drive people to your website. You still may need two or three touches before prospective patients make an appointment for the procedure, and that's what your website is for and what you'll accomplish with the right Call to Action (such as receive a free report, call with questions, or schedule a free consultation). But unlike the early-stage information gathering, your touches will be specific and will come in quick succession.

If you still have doubts, think about your own search behavior. Imagine you're considering protecting your home with a security system. What do you do first? You probably enter the general search term "home security system." You deliberately cast a wide net because you're on a mission to learn everything you can. You visit several websites to find out what's possible. What's the latest in security equipment? What level of security is adequate for your neighborhood? Do you need monitoring or just a really loud alarm to thwart the bad guys? Can you monitor your home remotely from your smartphone?

Once you have exhausted your questions, have your answers, and maybe even have spoken with your neighbors to find out what they're using, you're ready to commit. Again you search; only this time your search terms are more specific—more focused on finding an expert installer and monitoring service. Your search term might be: "Buy home security monitoring in Naples, FL" or "Best home security installer in Dallas, TX." You've changed the parameters of your search by using what's called a long-tail keyword phrase (three or more words in the search phrase). We'll get into this more in the traffic section. For now you just need to understand the difference and how by effectively targeting your ads to active buyers—as opposed to those who are simply curious—you can shorten your process and bring greater immediacy to the process. And according to Moz, the inbound marketing consultants, 70 percent of search traffic is built around long-tail keywords, with 5-word keywords being optimal. **Pay Per Click Paid Search ads target people who are ready to purchase and want the best option available.** Because you've optimized your ad by choosing the best long-tail keywords, you're going to have higher conversion rates. In other words, there's a better chance that someone will click through to your website and act on your Call to Action. Of course, after the clickthrough, your website still has to deliver.

Decision: While I've included this discussion here, your real decision will be to work with your ad traffic expert to select the right long-tail keyword phrases. We'll get into this more in the traffic section of the book.

Find Your Niche: Focus Your Message on One Thing

Even though your direct response campaign is designed to connect with prospective patients late in the buying cycle, you'll still need more than one touch. No one is going to buy surgical procedures or even Botox treatments from a PPC ad and a quick trip to your website—even if you add a shopping cart and a PayPal link.

Retail shopping may be part entertainment—like window shopping at the mall or browsing the aisles at WalMart or Best Buy. But when we're shopping for services, it's all business. With the right focus (the right message) on your website, you can satisfy a prospect's needs and have her saying, "Yes, now this is a physician who understands me. He clearly has a thorough knowledge of the procedure I want. This is exactly who I'm looking for. I want to know more. I'll call the office right now."

Think about it this way: You wouldn't go to a carpenter's website with the thought, *Hmm, maybe I could use a little carpentry work done. I wonder what this carpenter has to offer?* Similarly, when you call a carpenter over to talk about remodeling your living room, you don't want him to launch into a story about the great guesthouses he has built or the garages he has turned into game rooms. Service providers can't dump all the options on the table and invite prospects to pick something. Homeowners call a carpenter or a plumber or a CPA because they know *exactly* what they want. What they are searching for, however, is reassurance that the person they've found can do the job. Talking about guesthouses when the homeowners are asking about a living room remodel will leave them assuming he's not the right choice. They'll call another carpenter just as soon as they can usher this one out the door. It's the same in your profession.

"There's riches in niches."

For this reason we say, "There's riches in niches." It's the marketer's personal reminder to go small and stay focused...especially on the Internet. Chris Anderson, author of *The Long Tail*, wrote, "Increasingly, the mass marketing is turning into a mass of niches." Search engines enable even the smallest niches to find their audience, and that's exactly the audience you want—committed and ready to buy. Just as your Paid Search ads target with one message, so too must your website. Your Paid Search ads are not targeting plastic surgery junkies; they're bringing people with a specific need to your website with the promise of finding what they want. You need to ensure they are impressed with you by delivering on that promise. Author Susan Friedmann (*Riches in Niches*) says it best: "No matter what or whom we're talking about, from movies to chiropractors to books to financial planners, the consumer hankers after specialization."

Think about how you approach a patient in a face-to-face meeting. When Tom comes in for a consultation about his receding hairline and asks you if you can give him a natural head of hair again, what are you going to say? Surely not this:

> *"Oh certainly, Tom. I do hair transplantations regularly. In fact, I'm a full-service plastic surgeon. I also do as many breast augmentations every month. Oh, and let me tell you, my facelifts are world-renowned. I have done facelifts for royalty and half the Hollywood A-Listers. I'm the facelift king."*

Of course you wouldn't. It's exactly the same online. As soon as you start talking about other procedures to an audience that is focused on one particular procedure, you've lost them.

You've lost them, in part, because you're asking patients to do the work to figure out what you do and, in part, because every patient wants the reassurance that they're entrusting their bodies to a specialist.

Decision: Your goal is to find that one procedure you will talk about on your website. You're going to need business metrics to make the right choice. For now, I want you to make a clear distinction in your head between your practice and your marketing. In telling you to choose *one thing*, I'm NOT suggesting you change your medical practice or limit yourself in any way. This is not about your surgical center turning into the breast augmentation center or the hair transplantation center. Only your marketing needs to be niched. Not your practice. You can continue to offer the full range of plastic surgery procedures and treatments you always have. Keep doing your facelifts and breast augmentation and Botox injections and everything else. Just build a website that focuses on one (and only one) procedure.

Create the Right Perception: Present Yourself as the Expert

Everyone wants to hire an expert. So that's the perception you want to present. When you promote yourself as performing every cosmetic surgical procedure and offering every type of minimally invasive treatment, you'll be perceived as just another plastic surgeon. You'll be seen as a Jack-of-All-Trades when your prospective patient is looking for a Master of Liposuction or a Master of Hair Transplantation or a Master of Breast Augmentation. The more broadly you try to cast your marketing net, the fewer the number of people who will be interested. There's an inverse relationship between the range of skills you present and the perception of expertise.

Multiple Websites: 48% of Marketers Say "Yes"

When research firm MarketingSherpa asked marketers about their lead generation techniques, 48 percent reported that they build a separate website and landing page for every new marketing campaign. While you may decide to keep your brochure website of all the things you do, you shouldn't put a lot of money into it going forward—not if you're looking for greater ROI from your marketing efforts. Invest your time and money in small, highly targeted (niche) websites and the Paid Search ads that will drive traffic to these sites.

As you move forward with Emotional Direct Response Marketing, you're ultimately going to have multiple websites—one website per procedure that you wish to promote. Ultimately, your marketing budget will determine what you do. In our scenarios so far, we're talking about one site, but you could you go out and build 10 sites to promote all the different things that you do. Just be prepared to spend $50,000, $80,000, as much as $150,000 to build all the sites. And be prepared to spend $30,000, $60,000, even $100,000 a month to drive traffic to all the sites. If you're like most people, you will probably do one website/one niche at a time. As each becomes profitable, you start building the next.

Often I'm asked if the brochure site can serve as a central website that connects several niche sites. My best answer has to be maybe. We'll have to study this on an individual, case-by-case basis. There are so many nuances within SEO and the various ways of driving traffic to your site that affect whether or not you should link everything up.

Admit it, you're no different from your patients. If, God forbid, while you're reading this book, you start having heart palpitations and pain is radiating down your left arm and across your back, you have to consider the possibility that you're having a heart attack. You call an ambulance and ask them to have a cardiologist standing by at the hospital. When you get to the Emergency Room, you're not going to be happy if they put you on a gurney and say, "Listen we have a great plastic surgeon working the ER today, would you like to talk with her first?" You want an expert when you need an expert. And so does everyone else. Be that expert.

> You want an expert when you need an expert. And so does everyone else. Be that expert.

All things being equal, and assuming you and five other physicians in your community are licensed plastic surgeons with experience and good skills, who's the expert? The fact is, you're not the expert because you're the very best in the world. You're the expert because you're good at what you do AND you focus your message on the one subject a prospective patient wants addressed. When your website speaks to Sarah's issues better than anyone else's...when it answers her most burning questions...when it relieves her concerns and calms her fears...for Sarah, that makes you the expert to call. AdWords brought her to your site because your PPC ad promised to address her issues. It's up to you to prove your expertise.

If someone in Boca Raton wants a breast augmentation and there are five plastic surgeons in town (and four of them have brochure sites that emphasize the surgeons' range of skills) and if only Dr. Richards has a website that speaks exclusively about breast augmentation, who do you think is going to get the most appointments? No contest. Even before her first face-to-face consultation, Dr. Richards is perceived as more of an expert than everybody else because she has a whole website dedicated to breast augmentation.

Decision: Get comfortable with the notion of being the expert in a field of qualified professionals. And here's the real secret, when you post multiple websites—each focused on one particular procedure—you will be perceived as an expert in many fields. If Tom comes to you via your hair transplantation site, he'll perceive you to be the expert (and the best choice) for his procedure. Sarah, who found you through your breast augmentation site will perceive you as the expert in that procedure. With this understanding, you are ready to select your niche—the one procedure or treatment you will market first...your first area of expertise.

Analyze the Business Metrics: Determine the Lifetime Value of a Patient

So how do you pick a niche? It's not hard, but first you will need to analyze your practice in more detail than most people give to the task. Few people sit down and figure out what each of their products and/or services are worth and where they make the most money. To find the niche—the one thing—that your website and your marketing will focus on first, you need a thorough understanding of the metrics of each procedure.

One of the things I do when I meet with a client is ask them some questions. When I talk with physicians, my first question is, What is your most profitable procedure? Off the top of your head, you may say breast augmentation or rhinoplasty because you can charge on average $7,000 or $8,000 per procedure. But you may be surprised by what your analysis will show.

Profitability is actually determined by the **lifetime value of a patient**, which is another way of saying the return on investment (or ROI) of a procedure. In other words, to select a niche for your first direct response website, you need to understand your best revenue opportunities. Before we start, you need to appreciate the difference between a one-time procedure and the treatments that bring recurring revenue.

Lots of businesses have recurring revenue. Imagine for a minute that you own a supermarket and you're selling a wide range of items to people who come in and fill up their baskets. When they come back every few days (or even once a week) to buy more, that's recurring revenue. But to get new customers in the door, most retailers promote a series of special offers: a one-day sale on paper towels, discounts on select cuts of beef, buy-on-get-one (BOGO) free deals on cat food. These are loss-leaders, and if you're a retailer, you know that at best you may break even on these specials. You might even lose a little on the sale. Depending on the size of the discount, it might take three or four more visits before a new customer starts paying off. But retailers are willing to do this because they know that if a customer keeps returning they will make a profit.

> ...to select a niche for your first
> direct response website, you need to
> understand your best revenue
> opportunities.

When deciding how much to spend on these types of discounts and loss leaders, retailers need to figure out their overall business equation. They determine how much on average they will make through the years from a returning customer.

That's the lifetime value of a customer. They know exactly how much they can afford to lose up front to make X dollars profit in the course of, say, 5 years. The returning customer represents recurring revenue.

It's the same in your practice, only you may not run a lot of special discounts to get a new patient in the door. Instead, you should compare the lifetime value of a minimally invasive treatment (e.g., Botox, facial fillers, hair removal) with the one-time value of a surgical procedure. No one gets Botox once or facial fillers once. These are treatments that are repeated over and over again.

By the same token, few people need more than one rhinoplasty, augmentation mammaplasty, otoplasty or pectoral implant surgery. And those who do—the human Barbie dolls and the plastic surgery obsessed—have a unique set of issues and may not be your ideal patients.

As we look at the numbers, we find that major cosmetic surgery may cost a patient on average $7,000 or $8,000 (or more) for a procedure that requires two-and-a-half to three hours to perform. That's roughly $2,500 an hour, which is a nice payday. But then we have to ask, what's the likelihood that the patient who comes in for a rhinoplasty at age 18 will be back? Even if they decide to have breast augmentation surgery at age 33 or a facelift at age 40, what are the chances they'll be living in the same place and choose to come back to you?

Let's see how the ROI from recurring treatments of Botox compares with surgical procedures. First, we have a number of assumptions and costs that need to be factored into the equation. I've laid out our hypothetical example in a series of spreadsheets. This is only a hypothetical example, and your data and assumptions may differ from mine. That's all right. On the next page, you'll still see how to model your own calculations.

Average Lifetime Value of a Botox Patient	
Assumptions (Hypothetical)	
Average age of first visit	55 years old
Average age of last visit	78 years old
Total years as a patient	24
Gender differences	Men c. 20% more units per muscle
Wholesale cost per unit of Botox	$4
Average cost per unit to patient	$15
Average dilution	2cc
Average units lost (waste)	15 units
Average units per procedure	33
Average revenue per patient visit	$500
Average # patient visits/annually	3
Based on above assumptions, we know that:	
Average wholesale cost per visit	$132
Average net profit per visit	$368
Average annual net profit	$1,104
Lifetime Value of Patient	$26,496

Now as a skilled plastic surgeon, you can probably get much more granular in your analysis. For example, even though I gave an average dilution rate for the Botox powder, I didn't use that in my cost calculations. And my assumption about the amount of waste per vial (based on not using up an open vial within the first 24 hours, before it loses potency) is only a guess. But adding this variable to the list of assumptions may help you re-think your patient scheduling to gain greater efficiency. I also didn't take into consideration inflation and costs rising from year to year. And finally, while I'm assuming for the purposes of this exercise that a patient may continue to receive Botox injections for 24 years (from age 55 to age 78), I realize that this does not represent the lifetime value of every patient. Some will move away, others will start their treatments later in life, and some patients will die prematurely. So you'll need to come up with metrics that best fit your experience.

Even with my hypotheticals, estimates and potentially flawed assumptions, you can see that the lifetime value of a patient wanting recurring treatments can be significantly greater than the ROI from a one-time procedure—$8,000 versus $26,000—with one caveat: Is there a greater likelihood that a patient who comes to you for a blepharoplastic procedure or liposuction may come back in a few years for a rhytidectomy or abdominoplasty or upper arm lift? This is something to consider when analyzing your metrics.

Define Your Recurring Revenues Carefully

The possibility of repeat business from a one-time procedure reminds me of an example from my years in the mortgage business. I started in the business before the boom years and continued through and for a couple years after the big bust. Before the boom and bust, people were refinancing every three years. If I got somebody in a house, I was likely to get them back in three years—that qualifies as recurring revenue. But they wouldn't just come back because they'd been with me before; I had to continue marketing to them. And that's why you want to always be marketing.

After the boom and bust, marketing was absolutely imperative. By that time people had gone back to the traditional seven-year refinance cycle. That's comparable to a one-time customer; I could no longer assume that refinancing was a recurring revenue. In seven years a lot can happen. With marketing, I might get them back, but it was far from a sure thing. So I

con't

> couldn't afford to lose money on a client up front. The last thing I wanted to do was lose money on a client up front because seven years later I might get them back. Their lifetime value, while it might be a little bit higher than the initial transaction, it's not going to be dramatically higher.

Once you have your numbers, you can determine your most profitable procedure. But before you select a niche for your first Emotional Direct Response campaign, you have a couple more factors to consider. *First*, ask yourself if the most profitable procedure is something you want to sell because you can assume that as soon as you begin your direct response campaign you're going to be doing a lot more of these procedures. If it's not something you like—or want—to do then it's not a good fit. In which case, look at your next most profitable procedure and decide if this is a better option.

Second, you need to study your cash flow. Your direct response campaign is going to bring additional expenses beyond the costs you already incur in your practice. Some are upfront costs (e.g., initial marketing consulting, website design, copywriting) and others will be ongoing expenditures (e.g., ongoing consulting, hosting fees, ad buying, and monitoring/managing ad metrics). Your upfront, out-of-pocket costs might run $15,000, while your monthly costs could range from $1,500 to $3,000, and more as your ads are proven to work and you become more aggressive in buying your PPC keywords.

If you've been in business for a while and have good cash flow, you probably won't need to weigh your options as carefully. But if you need to pay for your direct response campaign out of new revenues, you may decide that getting the one-time, upfront payments from surgical procedures is a more financially viable option than waiting for the profits from recurring business to kick in. Let's look at two scenarios.

In our first example, let's say you choose to make breast augmentation your marketing niche. After spending $15,000 for your website, copywriting and initial consulting, you decide to start the year spending $3,000 a month on traffic to bring people to your website. As you can see from the spreadsheet below, you don't need many new patients to make a profit. And going forward, as your marketing professionals track and tweak your campaign and your results continue to improve, you decide to increase your traffic buys. Using my assumptions, you'll go from spending $3,000 a month on traffic to $6,000, and your total expenditures on marketing in your first year will be $60,000. That may sound like a lot to a physician not used to spending much on marketing, but you only need nine new patients a year to see a profit. And I've used some very conservative growth projections to reach an annual net profit of $283,000 from new breast augmentation patients. How many times would you do that? The answer is obvious: As many times as humanly possible. How many niche sites like that would you want? Again, as many as possible.

Emotional Direct Response Campaign -- Breast Augmentation					
	Costs			Profit	
	Up-front	Ongoing	# new patients	Gross	Net
Month 1	$15,000	$3,000	2	$14,000	-$4,000
Month 2		$3,000	2	$14,000	$11,000
Month 3		$3,000	3	$21,000	$18,000
Month 4		$3,000	3	$21,000	$18,000
Month 5		$3,000	3	$21,000	$18,000
Month 6		$3,000	4	$28,000	$25,000
Month 7		$3,000	4	$28,000	$25,000
Month 8		$3,000	4	$28,000	$25,000
Month 9		$3,000	4	$28,000	$25,000
Month 10		$6,000	6	$42,000	$36,000
Month 11		$6,000	6	$42,000	$36,000

	Up-front	Ongoing	New patients	Recurring visits	Gross	Net
Month 12		$6,000	8		$56,000	$50,000
TOTALS	$15,000	$45,000	49		$343,000	$283,000

Now let's look at a similar hypothetical for the recurring business from Botox treatments. I've used the same set of assumptions that I described earlier in this chapter. The net profit per visit is $368. As you can see, your profits in the first year are low. You break even, but just barely.

Emotional Direct Response Campaign -- Botox Year 1						
	Costs				Profit	
	Up-front	Ongoing	New patients	Recurring visits	Gross	Net
Month 1	$15,000	$3,000	4	0	$1,472	-$16,528
Month 2		$3,000	4	0	$1,472	-$1,528
Month 3		$3,000	6	2	$2,944	-$56
Month 4		$3,000	6	5	$4,048	$1,048
Month 5		$3,000	8	6	$5,152	$2,152
Month 6		$3,000	6	8	$5,152	$2,152
Month 7		$3,000	6	10	$5,888	$2,888
Month 8		$3,000	8	12	$7,360	$4,360
Month 9		$3,000	10	10	$7,360	$4,360
Month 10		$6,000	9	13	$8,096	$2,096
Month 11		$6,000	10	17	$9,936	$3,936
Month 12		$6,000	8	20	$10,304	$4,304
TOTALS	$15,000	$45,000	85	103	$69,184	$9,184

Emotional Direct Response Campaign -- Botox Year 2						
	Costs				Profit	
	Up-front	Ongoing	New patients	Recurring visits	Gross	Net

Month						
Month 1		$6,000	10	45	$20,240	$14,240
Month 2		$6,000	12	42	$19,872	$13,872
Month 3		$6,000	15	50	$23,920	$17,920
Month 4		$6,000	14	80	$34,592	$28,592
Month 5		$6,000	20	60	$29,440	$23,440
Month 6		$6,000	22	60	$30,176	$24,176
Month 7		$8,000	20	65	$31,280	$23,280
Month 8		$8,000	25	90	$42,320	$34,320
Month 9		$8,000	22	85	$39,376	$31,376
Month 10		$8,000	30	90	$44,160	$36,160
Month 11		$8,000	33	120	$56,304	$48,304
Month 12		$8,000	35	130	$60,720	$52,720
TOTALS	$0	$84,000	258	917	$432,400	$348,400

The interesting observation, however, is how dramatically profits grow in the second year as more of the recurring business kicks in. This is the power of compounding at work. In my hypothetical example, Botox treatments overtake breast augmentation in Year Two. But even if it takes you three years, the numbers are stunning. Clearly Botox treatments can be more profitable than breast augmentation surgery—both in terms of lifetime value of a patient and overall contribution to the growth of the practice. It's just not going to happen upfront. The recurring revenue campaign is front-end loaded with expenditures. But if your cash flow is otherwise good, you won't care. Even if it costs you $100 per patient in the first three months, you're going to make $1,500 per patient, minus your expenses, every year going forward. It's just going to take a little longer to pay off.

One final consideration. And this is going to be true whether you are running a campaign for one-time, up-front payments for surgical procedures or the recurring revenue from minimally invasive treatments. When you put together a campaign fully optimized for success with a focused website and strong emotional copywriting that performs—and when you drive highly targeted traffic to your website using long-tail keywords and continue to monitor and tweak elements of the campaign for the best possible results—your clickthrough rate will continue to rise. Google rewards your success with premium positions on the search results page and lower cost-per-click (CPC) rates on the keywords you want to buy. In this case, success really does breed success.

Decision: To choose a niche for your first marketing campaign, start with a thorough analysis of your business metrics. But your decision cannot be based solely on ROI. You need to weigh the numbers against the procedure or treatment you like best. And don't forget to factor in cash flow. Recurring revenue may be the winner in the long run, but if you need to boost revenues in the short term, you may need to choose a one-time surgical procedure for your first market niche. In which case, once the first campaign is turning a profit, you can go with a treatment for your second campaign that brings in recurring revenue.

Lifetime Value of a Patient: Another Way to Measure

There are many factors to consider when calculating the lifetime value of a patient. We've already compared the difference between a one-time surgical procedure like augmentation mammaplasty (average $8,000) versus recurring treatments of Botox (as much as $26,000).

Now let's consider the difference between an augmentation mammaplasty and blepharoplasty (the common eyelid lift). And here we need to take into consideration the age and long-term needs of the patient. The 30 year old who wants a breast augmentation may only be interested in improving her natural assets a bit. So she spends $8,000 for breast implants. For her, it's a one-time investment to feel better about her appearance. Possibly she's so pleased

con't

---

with the results, she comes back in a year or two for a rhinoplasty, which could earn you another $4,000. But assuming she doesn't go in for the full Barbie doll makeover, her lifetime value is around $12,000. That's a nice income, but...

Compare the first patient with a 50 year old who decides to have her eyelids lifted...she wants to freshen her look a bit. That goes well, and she feels confident in your skills—and those little laugh lines continue to grow deeper. So maybe she decides to invest in Botox treatments. In the course of the next 10 years, this patient might be worth another $11,000, at which time she decides to have a facelift (price tag about $8,000). And a year later, she asks you for a tummy tuck ($5,000). The lifetime value of this patient might go as high as $25,500. And to her, looking her best is...PRICELESS. This is, of course, completely hypothetical, but the potential is there, and you need to consider all the possibilities.

I'm not suggesting that you size up every patient who walks into your office this way. I'm only using these scenarios and running some hypothetical metrics to help you see the value of using business metrics to determine the best choice of marketing niche. As a marketer (not a physician) this is how we look at everything from a purely practical business perspective.

If You Think You're Selling a Procedure, Think Again!

You have a market niche. But what are you selling? I know you're too savvy now to tell me that you're a plastic surgeon with a full-service practice and that's what you're selling. But guess what, you're also not selling that one niche procedure. I know, this sounds counterintuitive, but let me explain.

...when you drive highly targeted traffic to your website using long-tail keywords and continue to monitor and tweak elements of the campaign for the best possible results—your clickthrough rate will continue to rise.

You're not selling hair transplants or breast augmentation surgery or even Botox treatments. Not from an AdWords ad and a website alone. Not unless you can show me that people come to your website and on the basis of some brilliant copywriting they are putting $7,000 or $8,000 procedures in their shopping carts and booking appointments online. So if you're not selling a procedure, what are you selling?

Create a Call to Action That Delivers

What you're selling on your website is an action that gets your prospective patients one giant step closer to booking an appointment for their procedure. Exactly what that action will be is something you have to figure out. This will be your **Call to Action**. Let me get you started by telling you what I think you should be selling, and you have several options. I'm going to tell you about three possible things to sell from your website, and the advantages of each one.

OPTION ONE—SELL AN APPOINTMENT FOR A CONSULTATION: Most physicians want a prospective patient to pick up the phone and call for a free consultation. The Call to Action is the phone call to book the free appointment.

So the first thing that people want to sell, and I think this is saleable and viable, is to sell an appointment. And it's usually a free appointment. Even though it's free, you still have to sell it. Somebody has to buy into the idea of picking up the phone and taking time out of the day to go see you.

They also need to follow through, not just think about it. They have to do it, and then they have to keep the appointment because in reality, did you actually sell an appointment or did you just sell a phone call to book an appointment? You sold a phone call. That's what the appointment is. That's your Call to Action. It's a little more complicated than that and more, but it's a phone call.

In its simplest form, the Call to Action might read: "Call for your free consult." Now, I don't like that Call to Action; it's what everyone else does. That's back to the old incestuous-marketing thing—everyone's doing it so I guess I should too…it must work. While we're okay with selling the phone call to get the appointment, we need to polish it up and make it shine. We want something more compelling, something that plays to those emotional issues that keep prospects on your site. That's a copywriting issue, but here's an example of what I mean: "Call for your free 'Wow, my breasts look great' strategy session." Now your pitching more than your free consultation; you're promoting the emotional benefit. Nobody's offering that, so it's different and makes you stand out. It's better. Is it great? No, because you're still selling a phone call.

OPTION TWO—START A CONVERSATION WITH THE PROSPECTIVE PATIENT: Start the conversation on your website by anticipating prospective patients' questions. Let them see you as

*the best source for information and expertise, which
will encourage them to take the next step. Your Call
to Action is the invitation to call to get more
information and start a conversation.*

If you have a good back office with people who can handle phone calls, you might change your Call to Action to read: "Pick up the phone today and ask us your questions...there's no obligation." Or, "Pick up the phone and talk to one of our beautiful breast strategists." That's even better.

But to do this, you must have a good back office in place. You need somebody who's scripted and informed and able to say, "Hi, my name is Gina. How may I help you beautify your breasts today? How can I make you become more confident about your figure?" Something like that. And she better be able to handle most any question because now she has to sell the appointment without forcing the issue. You want to make sure the caller keeps the appointment, and she won't show up if she feels coerced. That's a caller's greatest fear—that it's too hard to get questions answered without being forced to take the next step.

You can do a lot to calm these concerns by giving away a lot of good information on your website. The long-form sales letter on the landing page can do this by anticipating and answering a lot of questions, and the FAQ page is another place where you can answer questions. When you're seen as responsive and willing to answer questions, prospective patients will feel better about making the phone call. And there's an extra benefit: You and your staff will be answering fewer questions and probably have an easier time getting prospects to take the next step—coming in to meet the physician. If you do your site right, people will see you as the best source for the information they need to make a decision.

*OPTION THREE—SELL INFORMATION
THAT ANTICIPATES THE QUESTIONS AND
QUALIFIES YOUR LEADS: Whether your Call to
Action is a report or a video, whether it's free or you
charge a small fee, let your information pre-sell
prospects. With the promise of good information as
your Call to Action, you can raise your close rate.*

At the end of the day, what you really want to sell is information. In most cases, it's going to be free information, but you are still "selling" prospects on the need to take that information. The Call to Action is to take the information. The format could be a free report, which is really an extension of the sales letter on your landing page that sells them even better than your website does. There's a million different ways to write the report, but that's a whole separate training course on direct response copy. Your information could also be a free video. In either case, you'll need the help of an expert to write the report or script and produce the video.

Loading the front end with good information is definitely a stronger Call to Action than asking for a phone call to book a consultation or starting a conversation by inviting people to call with questions. That's especially true if you don't have a support staff that's up to the job.

The key is to choose a Call to Action that gets results. This is critical because the more people who take your report, the more calls you get, the more appointments you'll book, and the more people you can get in front of, the more procedures you'll sell. So we definitely want people to call; it's just a matter of choosing the best tactics for your market.

A Call to Action is Not Always Free

While most people offer free reports, there is another school of thought. Let me say right up front that getting prospective patients to pay for your information is harder than giving away a free report. It's also a more complicated process that requires more steps—both for you and your prospects. But it can be a better overall marketing strategy because it further qualifies a prospect, and in the end that's what you really want. Let me explain.

Other than prospects' concerns that they may get forced into a face-to-face consultation when they call your office for information, their obligation is minimal when they can browse your website, download a free report, or call the office to ask a few questions. **Buying a report or a video is a commitment.** Even a nominal fee is a huge step forward psychologically. By the same token, making such a commitment will weed out the merely curious.

From the standpoint of your time, you really only want the most committed prospects booking free consultations with you. You're making $250 to $300 an hour—more when you're in surgery—so allocate your time (and that of your staff) wisely. While marketing is a numbers game, it's also about doing everything you can to raise the quality of your leads, which is what optimization is all about. Do you want to spend half your day selling when you should be performing surgeries and treatments? No, and you certainly don't want to use your time talking to people that you can't sell?

So here's one last metric for you to consider: What's your conversion rate right now? Of the people who walk in the door and you meet for a consult, what percent do you close (in other words sell)? That's something that you need to know. Let's say you're amazing and you close 50 percent of your consults. You probably aren't closing at 80 percent. But what if you could? What if the only people who come to see you are already pre-sold to buy from you? They're just coming in to meet their physician face to face, ask a few questions and give you a chance to do a pre-operative evaluation. Basically, they're meeting you because they've already decided they want you as their plastic surgeon.

Again, nobody's buying a breast augmentation or a hair transplantation or even Botox from a report (fee or free). But charging a small amount to take the next step can increase your closing ratios so that now practically everyone you meet already wants you as their physician. And in truth, most of the 20 percent or so that you're not booking, you're probably turning away. Maybe they have unrealistic expectations or you can't really help them or it's not something you even want to do.

Decision: The right Call to Action will increase your closing ratio. Based on your current closing ratio and your cash flow, you need to decide what you want prospects to do once they are on your website. If you only want highly qualified prospects calling for consults, make the website and your Call to Action pre-sell them. Just remember that the more steps you put in place, the fewer people will follow through with you...but those who do will be more likely to schedule a pre-operative consultation and agree to hiring you as their physician. It's a trade off. While only a third of people may follow through, maybe you'll close 80 percent to 90 percent.

Whatever you choose to do, tracking the results going forward remains critical. Similarly, if you opt to start a conversation with prospects and invite them to speak with your staff, you'll want to pay attention to their questions. If everyone asks the same thing, maybe it's time to include the answer on your FAQ page. This simple change will automate one more step and save staff time. If you're booked three months in advance, you'll probably want to make this clear so you're not getting 10 phone calls a day from people who expect to have their surgery tomorrow. If you find that not enough people are calling for consultations and you want to spend more of your time selling, then make the Call to Action easier. Instead of a report, invite them to call immediately for their "Beautiful Breast Consultation."

Now you're ready to analyze your own metrics and make the critical decisions that will determine not only the focus of your website but the components of your direct response campaign. Select your niche, position yourself as the expert, set your Paid Search ads to appear late in the sales cycle, choose the right Call to Action and limit your time to those appointments most likely to be pre-sold on your expertise. Do this right and you may soon be booked out a year or two in advance. If that happens and if you only do 25 surgical procedures a month, but you have 50 people calling that want procedures with you, you'll definitely be raising your prices. If for no other reason than there's a whole lot less of you to go around.

It all starts with you knowing your business and deciding what you want to do. Let's start building a website.

Chapter 3
Market Rules!
Use Your Market to Focus
Your Message and Media!

*"Think big and don't listen to people
who tell you it can't be done.
Life's too short to think small."*

– Tim Ferriss, *author of* The 4-Hour Workweek

A t this point, you should understand the basics of working through your business metrics, calculating the lifetime value of a patient, and picking a specific procedure (niche). You can't optimize unless you first know what you're trying to do...and why. These are the critical steps to any set up. So if you haven't worked through them, if you've jumped ahead to this section, you need to go back to Chapter 2 and make these business decisions.

As you now prepare to develop your Emotional Direct Response campaign, write copy and design a website, your focus is procedural. You're about to work your way through your **MARKET, MESSAGE** and **MEDIA**. And with apologies to Marshall McLuhan and his 1964 pronouncement that "the medium is the message," when it comes to marketing, the MARKET IS THE MESSAGE. Or at least the market guides the message. I'll explain why.

But first, a reminder: We've talked about incestuous marketing and why it's the wrong approach. And how it's the trap we fall into when we don't understand how good marketing works. While copying the approach of others may seem to be the natural and intuitive path, the results can be disastrous. There's nothing strategic about following in the footsteps of generations of business owners who have all approached their marketing the same way. With my help, you're optimizing for success.

In this chapter, we're going to explore the elements needed to build a powerful, focused website that is optimized for results. But this is not going to be a nuts-and-bolts approach. I'm not showing you step-by-step how to build a site using the WordPress platform. That's what you hire professionals for. As the author Aldous Huxley once explained, "It is far easier to write 10 passably effective sonnets than one effective advertisement." Because he's right, I want you to understand how to make Emotional Direct Response Marketing work on your website, but hire a copywriter and website designer who can deliver the results you want.

Better still, work with a strategic direct response-marketing consultant who has access to all the expert talent you need. Yes, that's someone like me. No, actually, it is me, and I'm going to show you why. In the interest of total transparency and full disclosure, I'm even going to show you how I would put together a campaign to sell my services...to you!

75

So, How Much Money Do You Have to Spend?

Yes, I know, that sounds a little creepy. And it should, which is why you won't hear most agency types say it quite so blatantly. But that's exactly what they want to know. The reason is, they want to figure out which types of media best match your budget. To a typical ad or marketing rep the media is irrelevant although the choice does impact their bottom line. The payday on placing television ads is usually greater than that from placing banner ads on websites, developing Paid Search campaigns or even buying ad space in a magazine or local newspaper. I have to say "usually" because if you buy enough placements, you can spend a lot on any campaign.

While the rep does have a vested interest in his or her own bottom line—and like you wants to make money—many do want to get you the best bang for the buck. That's their nod to giving you a good return on investment. But here's the problem: Their definition of "bang" is different from yours. They're thinking in terms of the media placement and not the overall campaign strategy. They're not results oriented...at least not in the sense that they will tell you that they can deliver sales or increase your ROI by running one kind of promotion versus another. They talk in terms of "eyeballs."

By way of explanation, let me share a little story. My wife Wendy and I were out to dinner with friends, and they brought along another couple—some friends of theirs. As we all got to talking, the woman (their friend) said she was a rep for an ad agency, which meant she sold media—Internet, magazines, direct mail, radio, billboards, television, the whole media megillah. Her job was to deliver a client's message via whatever media outlet the client could afford. Our conversation went something like this:

"I'm a rep for so-and-so agency," she said.

"You know the problem with agencies," I replied, "none of you track results for clients."

"What do you mean? How can we track results?"

"You're kidding me, right? I can tell you a million different ways to track results. For example, put a dedicated phone number in an advertisement, and if you have three different ads running, you run three different calls to action with different phone numbers. You'll quickly know which approach is working best."

"Oh, we don't do that," she said.

At that point, I went for the jugular. "The reason you don't do that is you don't want anybody to know your results."

And that's when her husband jumped in. "They're only promising you eyeballs. That's the only thing they're promising."

I couldn't resist. "Well, it's not *really* all they're promising—or at least implying that they're promising. If it's only eyeballs, I don't need them. And no one else does either. Anyone can go directly to a magazine and buy ad space or to a network or radio station and buy time. Businesses don't need an agency to do that. If all you're doing is buying eyeballs, well I can buy them myself. There's an expectation that you have the expertise that's going to help someone make money. That's your implied promise."

Actually my last statement is only half true. Anyone can buy ad space or time although most business owners don't realize how easy it is to do. Nor do they understand the implication of buying eyeballs. The real issue is whether or not they're buying the RIGHT eyeballs. Plus, most business owners, service professionals (including physicians) think agencies are delivering brilliant creative that will bring them results in the form of customers, clients and patients. In reality, they're falling for the trap that is cornerstone of brand advertising, and as we've discussed, that's not direct response (let alone Emotional Direct Response) marketing. Branding is not focused on immediate results. It's entertainment. Think Super Bowl ads. Although they represent the big-dollar, high-end of the market, the analogy holds for all brand advertising. Think about your own reaction to Super Bowl ads. You watch to be entertained—the more clever and funnier, the better. You're not watching because you can't wait to see all the new products that you'll rush out on Monday morning to buy.

The proof is in the pitch you get when an agency is trying to win your business. They tell you that the reason you should hire them is because they've won all kinds of awards for their creative (that's the implied promise that you're buying a brilliant creative strategy). **But the awards are NOT for ROI.** They don't tell you how they won an award for getting their clients a 1,527 percent return on investment. Nor will they say that for every $1,000 their clients spend, they typically get $30,000 back. They don't say that because they can't. Even on the chance that it might occasionally be true, they won't tell you because they honestly don't know...because they don't track results.

The truth is, one media isn't better per se than another. Each is only as good as it's ability to help you reach your intended audience (your target market) and deliver results. Sales. And patients. But ask any ad or marketing agency to give you specific results and information on how they track results, and all you're going to get is a blank look. And the whole problem stems from the fact that their primary interest is in the media—and what a client can afford to buy. They're coming at the whole problem backwards.

So I'm not going to ask you, "What's your budget?" What I am doing with this book, however, is giving you enough information to focus your objectives and set your budget realistically. The nice thing about PPC Paid Search is you control exactly how much you spend. **So the question I will ask you to consider is this: "What are you willing to spend to get a customer?"**

Market-Message-Media...In That Order!

My mentor, copywriting genius Dan Kennedy, distills direct response down to a three-pronged trilogy: Market, Message and Media. It's the who, what (how), and where of marketing. You start with your MARKET by asking, to whom am I selling? Once you know the who, you can focus on the MESSAGE. What do I want to say and how do I want to say it? Only then do you think about the MEDIA. Where does my target market hang out to read/watch/consume content?

When building a direct response marketing campaign, your first decision is never to choose a media. You don't start by choosing the Yellow Pages, for example, because you think you can afford that, or selecting your local newspaper because you like reading the paper, or opting for radio because some rep just offered you a good deal on a 15-second ad to run during the evening commute hours. No, you have to ask, "Where's my market most likely to be found?" This is what drives your choice of media. Not budget. Not convenience. Not a personal preference.

Let me put this in perspective: Working through your market, message and media is like any other business decision. It must make sense...and there must be a market before anything else can happen.

Let me put this in perspective: Working through your market, message and media is like any other business decision. It must make sense...and there must be a market before anything else can happen. Maybe this analogy will help you see the flaw in making a business decision for the wrong reasons:

When I was in the mortgage business and looking at other ways to make money, I came across a real estate promoter selling a turnkey business opportunity to buy property for pennies on the dollar. His program centered on investing in real estate by purchasing the liens on property with taxes in arrears. In principle, you buy the tax lien, wait 24 months, and at the end of that time and if the taxes have not been paid, you petition the court for the property. Although the ease of getting the property will vary from state to state, it's a great investment because 1) most states pay an obscene interest rate on your money (some places it's as high as 18 percent a year) and 2) it's the most secure investment you can have because real estate taxes are first lien. Nothing—not even the IRS—gets paid before real estate taxes. Even if the house burns down, you're getting paid. So you're in, say, for $15,000 worth of back taxes, you get paid first, the interest is excellent, and even if you end up receiving raw land it's probably worth more than the tax bill you paid.

But here's the problem. Unlike stocks and bonds, which you can sell to the public and make a commission, no one sells tax liens that way. So unless you wanted to invest in the liens yourself, there is no market to sell these liens to other people.

It's the same problem with selecting your media before you know your market and message. You may just end up with a campaign that no one sees. If your market is single women who want a breast augmentation, you begin by identifying their demographics: women of a certain age with certain backgrounds, certain incomes. But you also know something about her motivations, her behavior and interests. These are the psychographics, and they provide a much deeper insight into the type of message that will resonate. They also help you identify her media preferences.

Enter our hypothetical patient Sarah. She is the model for your market—women who are considering breast augmentation. Sarah is 27 years old. She has a mid-level office job in the city. She's not married and harbors some self-doubts about her image. Sarah dreams about looking sensational in a bikini. She reads *Vogue* magazine and spends time on the Internet searching and researching the pros and cons of plastic surgery. Sarah is *not* into videogames.

Now if you had begun the creative process by writing and designing an awesome ad to appear on Microsoft's Xbox One platform, it wouldn't matter that you had just created the greatest Xbox ad ever. Sarah is never going to see it, nor are 99 percent of the women in your ideal market. They're like Sarah and don't particularly enjoy videogames. Xbox is the wrong media for your market—Sarah and people like her looking for breast augmentation.

Be warned: If you find yourself talking with an agency, the market has to be your first topic of discussion. If they can't answer your questions or work with you to develop the demographics and psychographics for that market, run (don't walk) to the nearest exit. Then contact a direct response expert strategist with a market-centric approach who can consult with you. Someone who is paid to give you results...not media...not eyeballs. You've already settled on a niche for the right business reasons. Now you need to identify the market that is right for your niche.

The Market—Understanding Who You're Selling To

While your niche is going to help you identify your market, it's not enough to say, "I want to sell to people who love to play videogames. As Dan Kennedy explains in his marketing programs, "The goal is understanding. To persuade someone, to motivate someone, to sell someone, you really need to understand that person."

So let's take videogame fans. Among the real fanatics is a group that we'll call techno-geeks. So who are they? Well, to start, and I know this is a bit of a stereotype, they're primarily males between the ages of 15 and 30. They're both single and married. That's a very quick look at their demographics. They're psychographics can tell us more about their media tastes. Techno-geeks are real digital-philes. They don't read conventional, old-media, print newspapers. That's so 20th century. They're motivated by a desire to be on the cutting edge and working in real time. If they want news, they're getting it online. They're not into print magazines either. They probably read some direct mail, but only because it's still coming through the mail to their homes. If techno-geeks are our market, we must craft a message that speaks to them and place it on the Internet as digital media—on a web page where they are most likely to see the ad and read/hear/view our offer.

When we talk about a market's **demographics**, we're looking at where a group of people fit within the larger human population. We're looking for data that identify our market by age, gender, income, geographic location, employment and education. Assuming you're already performing the procedure or treatment that you've chosen as your marketing niche, you should be able to create a demographic profile of your market based on what you know about past patients.

Let's take Tom, our hypothetical patient for hair transplantation. If your practice is located in Connecticut, which is going to focus the geographic location of your market, you might tell me that Tom and your market for hair transplantation are married, single and divorced males between the ages of 45 and 60. They live in an affluent suburb in Fairfield County, have high profile jobs that require them to want to look their best—professional men, media persons, corporate executives. If they're not married, they may be dating and fearful that thinning or receding hair makes them look older than their years.

With a partial picture of Tom and his cohorts, what can you say about their attitudes, values, interests, activities and lifestyle? The study of psychographics dates to the 1960s when marketers found they could better predict customer behavior by looking beyond demographics. In the late 70s, social scientist Arnold Mitchell, then a researcher at SRI International, developed one of the best known analytical tools—VALS™ (Values, Attitudes and Lifestyles). Mitchell divided individuals into nine groups according to their social (external) values: Survivors, Sustainers, Belongers, Emulators, Achievers, I-Am-Me, Experientials, Socially Conscious and Integrateds. He defined the beliefs, motivations and attitudes for each group. Later Strategic Business Insights (SBI) refocused VALS on psychological (internal) variables, which have the advantage of remaining more constant over time than social values.

Tom's psychographics might look like this: As a Baby Boomer who loves sports cars, cares about the environment and is into all types of outdoor activities, Tom is an Achiever who strives to be at the top of his field and the best at everything he does. He'd rather surf and bungee jump than squirrel away in the house building ship models or listening to classical music. You'll find him watching extreme-sports videos and reading up on the latest attachments for his GoPro videocamera. To stay active, he lives a healthy lifestyle, eats organic foods and goes to the gym at least three times a week. And because he's back in the dating scene, he's become self-conscious about his thinning hair. With his lifestyle choices, a hairpiece won't cut it. He wants a more youthful look that he believes only a full head of hair will give him.

Admittedly this is not a scientific analysis. But for the purposes of copywriting, would this sort of profile give you enough insight to craft a message with a promise that would appeal to Tom and men like him? You bet.

The Message: Writing Headlines that Demand Attention

Every marketer and copywriter who knows his or her business will tell you the same thing: Your headline is the most important part of your message. As the copywriting superstar David Ogilvy, often called "The Father of Advertising," wrote decades ago, "The headline is the 'ticket on the meat.' Use it to flag down readers who are prospects for the kind of product you're advertising."

Headlines are the secret behind the success of publications like *National Enquirer*, *Cosmopolitan* and *People*. I don't care whether you buy them or not, you have read every single one of those covers while standing in the checkout line or sitting in a waiting room. The headlines draw you in, which is why their editors spend a fortune on writers who can create the best, the most compelling headlines. *National Enquirer* has changed its content in recent years and moved away from the "baby born with 13 heads" types of stories or my personal favorite from the old *Weekly World News*: "Bigfoot Kept Lumberjack as Love Slave." What has never changed is their ability to captivate readers with headlines. Here are a few simple examples; I've left

off the celebrity names attached to these stories (replaced with *
* *) and focused on the message:

"* * * Pregnant Again!"

"* * * Breaks Her Silence"

"* * * ONLY 4 Years to Live"

"* * * Forbidden to Cuddle New Baby—Unless...!"

You can't help but want to read more.

As we discussed in Chapter 1, you only have 3 seconds to
grab someone's attention. You have to have optimal impact in
these 3 seconds. As Copyblogger founder Brian Clark reminds us,
80 percent of people never read past the headline. That means
that at least 80 percent of your ability to be effective rests with
the headline. According to Peter Koechley—co-founder and
Curator-in-Chief of the social, viral media website platform
Upworthy—your web traffic can vary by as much as 500 percent
all based on your headline. So make your headlines count.

Good headline writing takes talent. But perhaps even
more important it takes focusing on the wants, dreams, fears and
secrets of your market. You don't have to be wildly creative as
much as you have to be compelling. You don't have to make crazy
offers—just the exact, right offer. Think of your headline as the
promise that your market has been waiting for, but to get it right
you need to know as much about your market as possible. And as
I've said before, the promise isn't you. So restrain any desire to
insert yourself, your practice, or surgical center into the headline.
In spite of your education, training and experience, you are not
the message. Not yet. Not until after you've made a connection.

And by the way, beautiful pictures, while nice, can't make
up for a bad headline. A picture of an attractive woman and your
name in the headline does not cause a woman to pick up the
phone and say, "I want you to do my breast augmentation." She

might think, *I want to look like her*, and the inference is that you can do that, but so can every other physician who has a photograph of a pretty face or a voluptuous figure on their website. She won't take the next step any more than a man will call for a hair transplantation consult simply because you have a photograph of a handsome man surrounded by adoring women.

We talked about using information to pre-sell a prospective patient. Well the pre-selling begins with the headline, which is why I spend more time developing headlines for my clients than writing the copy. The headline sets the tone. Sarah reads the headline and immediately she knows you're going to give her bigger breasts and boost her self-esteem. "I'm in," she says. "Tell me more." But "I'm Dr. Jones. I do breast surgery. Give me a call" is a big, fat zero.

As the late, legendary salesman Zig Ziglar explained, "People don't buy for logical reasons. They buy for emotional reasons." We talked about that earlier. They buy from emotion and justify their decision with logic. It is not logical for a person to want a physician to cut into her chest and insert silicone pillows up under her breasts. But it is very much an emotional decision to say, "I'm not happy with the way I look. I wish I had larger, firmer breasts that will get me noticed and make me beautiful." To women who feel this way, breast augmentation surgery is a viable, logical solution to a real problem.

There's a rule all writers live by: **Show, don't tell.** It'll make sense when I show you a few examples, but it's not always the easiest thing to do, and another reason why you want a pro writing your copy. The point is you need to SHOW her in your headline that you know what she's feeling...that you empathize and have a solution. Here's the difference:

TELL: In 25 Years of Practice, Dr. Jones Has Helped 1000s of Women Feel Better About Their Appearance.

SHOW:Stop Dreaming! You Can Have a Beach Body. Start Today with Your Free "Guide to Beautiful Breasts."

Telling someone what's possible sounds too clinical...you too can be one of 1000s served. It reads more like an old McDonald's sign..."Over 3 Billion Served." There's no warmth, no connection. It's more about Dr. Jones than the prospective patient who has a very secret dream. On the other hand, the "showing" version speaks directly to every woman who visits the website. By acknowledging her dream, you PROVE that you understand and offer the PROMISE of help...help that can start today.

And here's a headline that might get Tom to give your website a closer read and move him to take action and call: "Do you long for the days when women ran their fingers through your hair? Good News! Your best days may still be ahead."

Don't Guess, Test Your Headlines

You have so much riding on your headline that you want to get it right. TEST. And a great way to test a headline is to put up a site with just a headline and a phone number. Will that get somebody to pick up the phone and call? "If You Hate Looking in the Mirror, Call..." If a headline works on its own, you have a great message. This is not a replacement for a landing page and a sales letter. You aren't using this to sell them anything. All you want to find out is whether or not your headline is compelling enough to get someone to call. Pay Per Click ads is another great place to test headlines.

The Message—Making a Promise They Can't Refuse

If your prospective patients are still with you at this point and starting to read your sales letter, congratulations! You beat the 3-

second barrier. They're with you and want to know more. Now you need to build on the promise.

At this point, I know you're itching to start telling readers your story. Not yet! Curb your instincts and stay the course. You'll have ample opportunity on the About Us page to share your pedigree and tell them about your knowledge, expertise and experience. Right now you need to stay focused on the needs and emotions of your prospects. The more you can pre-sell them through your website, the more likely they are to take the next step with you. Your long-form sales letter needs to:

1) **Keep on Point.** Don't wander away from talking about the procedure or treatment (the niche) you're marketing. It's that procedure that brought them to your website in the first place...that and the promise of your headline. Use your copy to deliver on the promise you made. Build on it by heaping on the benefits. Answer the questions you know prospective patients have. Optimize your website by making yourself irresistible to prospects by doing a better job than anyone else in presenting the procedure they clearly want.

Not only are you focused on one niche, you're also focused on one market. It's the person you want sitting across from you in your office discussing her or his procedure or course of treatment. While thousands may read your copy, you're speaking to one person at a time. The woman with self-doubts about her figure who wants breast augmentation. The single man who fears that his receding hairline makes him look older and less desirable to women. The mother who knows that after several pregnancies her body hasn't bounced back and wants a tummy tuck. The mid-level manager who deserves a promotion but worries that with a wrinkled brow, deep laugh lines and a few crow's feet he can't compete with the younger guys.

2) Speak to Your Prospects' Issues. Your clients do care about who you are, but they care even more about their own issues. As John C. Maxwell, author of *The 21 Irrefutable Laws of Leadership*, wrote, "They don't care how much you know until they know how much you care." They'll know you care because you are talking about them and what they want.

Actually, let me amend this rule just a little. You can tell your prospects tons about yourself when you write about what prospects want to know. In other words, you can show your knowledge, your expertise and your experience by SHOWING that you understand the people who come to your page.

- **Show** that you know what your prospective patients are feeling by speaking to their anxieties.

- **Show** that you appreciate their fears by helping to calm their apprehension.

- **Show** that you respect their self-doubts by taking them seriously and making them feel better about themselves.

- **Show** them that they've found the right physician by answering their questions.

Showing is always better than telling. Think of this exercise as the greatest example of bedside manner, ever.

3) Maintain Your Emotional Tone. Your headline made an initial connection with your audience; don't lose them now. Build on that. Don't go all clinical on them. As the popular motivational and business speaker Les Brown puts it, "If you only talk to a person's head and not their heart people won't listen to you." You've been listening to patients for years; use what you know to build a deep emotional bond. If you have stories that will give prospective patients hope, share these to build confidence and tell them what they need to know.

A long-form sales letter is all about selling...with a twist. You're not the stereotypical used-car salesman brow-beating a customer into a sale. You're a compassionate professional who can help. That's how you pre-sell. Make them *feel* that they need to take the next step and act on your Call to Action to get the satisfaction they desire.

This is a job for a kick-ass copywriter. And just as you have years and hundreds of thousands of dollars invested in your profession, so do copywriters. Okay, we only have tens of thousands of dollars invested (not an exaggeration) but it takes years of writing and rewriting to do this well. Hire a good copywriter who understands the Emotional Direct Response sell, then work closely with him or her to provide the insight, the answers, the stories that are part of your experience. This is money well spent.

The Message: Tying Your Call to Action to What You're Really Selling

Since you want to do as much as possible to pre-sell your prospective patients, there's one more component to consider: what you're really trying to sell on your website. Your Call to Action isn't selling procedures; it's selling the next step that you want a prospective patient to take. And this offer needs to appear on every page of your website.

Whether you're offering people a digital download of a free report, a video, or the opportunity to get their questions answered by calling your office, maintain the same emotional tone in your Call to Action—with one difference. By now you're breaking through the barriers imposed by the lizard and limbic brains, so you can weave more facts and figures into your message. The neocortex is starting to pay attention.

The real purpose of your Call to Action is to get prospects to take the next step...to get them to buy in to your message. When you take prospects through enough steps and provide good information throughout, by the time they are ready to schedule a consult you are sitting down to talk with a person who is ready to be your patient. You want to do everything you can to narrow the field to people who really want plastic surgery and believe you are the person to perform the procedure.

The Media: Putting Your Message Where Your Market Is

While we're going get more into the media in our next chapter, I need to clear something up right now. I've already stressed that the problem when working with an agency is their heavy focus on media—without any discussion of your niche, market, or message. And that's true. But from the beginning of this book I've emphasized that your Emotional Direct Response Marketing campaign would use Google PPC Paid Search to drive traffic to your website. Did I just break my own rule and put the media first?

It's a fair question, and I have an answer. In principle, everything I've talked about in this book can be made to work with any media. You'll need to make some minor adjustments depending on the media. Television ad campaigns differ somewhat from print (magazine and newspaper) campaigns, which also differ from direct mail, and so on.

But there's more, and I'm going to call it proof in numbers. Internet advertising has grown rapidly in the last five or six years. The ad spend on Paid Search has been growing at a rate of between 12 percent and 18 percent annually, and both Forrester Research and marketing agency Zenith Optimedia estimate that US businesses will spend almost $58 billion on search marketing and Paid Search in 2014. That's about 48 percent of the total online advertising spend. The biggest recipient of those dollars is Google with 73 percent of marketers using Google AdWords campaigns. Microsoft's Bing is a distant second at 55 percent (the total is greater than 100 percent because some people run ads on multiple search platforms.)

When Hanapin Marketing surveyed marketing managers about their online advertising for its 2013 report, *The State of Paid Search*, 95 percent of participants said that text ads are "important" or "very important" to their business, and 83 percent reported that they feel "good" or "very good" about the current Pay Per Click market. It's hard to argue with success.

When it comes to return on investment, in 2010 the Direct Marketing Association (DMA) published a report entitled *The Power of Direct Marketing*. They looked at direct marketing results across different media and found that Internet Search has a higher ROI than every media except commercial email. The DMA estimated that every dollar spent on Internet search in 2014 would return $21.93; the average ROI across all direct marketing advertising is just $12.61.

As you'll see from my own story in the next section, I discovered the incredible power of Pay Per Click much the way you are now. A few people who had already used Paid Search and built high-converting websites pointed me in the right direction. I've used Paid Search to build my business, and now so can you.

While we've discussed the importance of identifying (and understanding) your market and crafting your message with your market in mind, the fact is targeting a market is always difficult. With Paid Search we enable interested prospects to target themselves. As David Meerman Scott wrote in the preface of the third edition of *The New Rules of Marketing & PR*: "Before the web came along, there were only three ways to get noticed: buy expensive advertising, beg the mainstream media to tell your story for you, or hire a huge sales staff to bug people one at a time about your products. Now we have a better option." While Scott goes on to talk about content publishing, what he's saying is equally applicable to Paid Search advertising. The Internet is that better option, and with Paid Search we're putting the prospective patient in control of the process.

Just as the Internet has put the power of publishing into the hands of authors and the distribution of music and videos within reach of anyone with a computer, so too Paid Search puts every business owner, service professional, physician, attorney (indeed everyone) in control of their advertising. While you control your message, which keywords you want to use, and how much you want to spend, ultimately you cede control to your prospective patients. Only when their choice of search terms matches your choice of keywords does your ad appear. Remember, early on I said that Paid Search was not a pure outbound advertising strategy because the market self-selects. They decide what they're searching for and choose the keywords they want to use to define their search. Given that almost 90 percent of consumers go to a search engine to find information about products and service before buying, Paid Search becomes the logical choice.

> ...Paid Search puts every business owner, service professional, physician, attorney (indeed everyone) in control of their advertising.

Finally, Paid Search removes many of the problems and challenges of SEO (search engine optimization) and organic search. Since NetMarketShare reports that 75 percent of people searching a subject never click past the first page of results, you need a strategy that puts you on page one. If you've spent any time trying to get your website to come up on page one of Google for keywords like "plastic surgery" or "Botox" or "breast augmentation," you know how difficult this can be. Pay Per Click can put you on page one. There is no more cost-effective way to reach a highly targeted market of people interested in having the procedures and treatments that you offer. And as physicians you have a wide-open market because out of the total digital ad spend, healthcare and pharmaceutical account for just 2.8 percent (eMarketer, August 2013). Now is your opportunity to act...before your competition reads this book and wakes up to the possibilities of Paid Search.

How I Learned to Sell Online

I ran a very successful mortgage business in New York for about 14 years—long before the boom and bust. I built much of it through marketing, although at the time I didn't know much more about marketing than you. In truth, by this point in your reading you know a lot more than I did back then. I found one or two marketing pieces that worked well, and I rode those things until they stopped working. The problem was when they stopped working I had no idea what to do next. I had no strategy and just did the whole incestuous marketing thing. Then I found Brian Sacks, who was a marketing guru to the mortgage industry, and he was my introduction to Emotional Direct Response Marketing and how to develop multi-step campaigns.

With his techniques, I was able to build my practice back up, right up to the big mortgage bust. My marketing continued to work during the bust, but it became much harder. I had to do a lot more face-to-face selling, whereas before I focused on marketing and my salespeople (who were really hired as glorified order takers) did the face-to-face stuff. I could see that I was going to have to do more of the selling and, frankly, I didn't want to do it. I needed a new business.

The timing couldn't have been worse. Wendy was pregnant with our first child, and we'd just bought an $800,000 house. I had big financial responsibilities, so I had to build a business...fast. This was five or six years ago.

I was looking for a solution, and the Internet at that time was still a little bit of a wild west, but it was also intriguing. I bought my first course from Internet marketer Ryan Deiss, called *Your First $1000*. The program is not available today, in large part because the model is no longer viable, but it taught me a lot. Ryan showed me how to build an information product by first figuring out what the market wants. His premise was that before you can make $1 million, you have to make $1,000. In other words, you have to learn to crawl then stand, before you can walk.

So I followed his structure, which was brilliant, and I had to do two things: find a market and something to sell. Instead of saying, "I'm in the mortgage business so I think that people in the mortgage business could use a coach right now, so I'll sell coaching services," I had to find my affinity—something I liked. Then I had to determine if there was a market, and Ryan taught me how to figure that out. I needed to find an existing product (someone else's product), become an affiliate and send traffic to that product. This is much harder to do today, but back then Google gave you a lot of latitude.

I was interested in hypnosis and found a site that was selling hypnosis products. I followed Ryan's steps and started to drive traffic to that site. People were buying, and I was making a profit. I think I made 50 percent on what was roughly a $100 item. Ryan's idea was that if I could sell someone else's product and make a profit, I could certainly develop and sell my own products and make a profit. Going the affiliate route was a safe way to test the market and determine if it had legs. The idea is just because somebody has something to sell on their website doesn't mean they're selling anything. It could be a bad market. So that's how Ryan taught me to determine my market.

Within six months I had built a $40,000-a-month business selling e-books, DVDs, videos and memberships. I was spending about $20,000 a month on Google AdWords (a $20,000 per month profit). It was a great way to test a market and build a business.

The wild-west days didn't last. The industry matured, and Google began to change the rules as to what you could and couldn't do. It put a crimp in my original business model, but by then I'd learned about markets and messages and how to build an online business, and I could move forward. Actually my hypnosis business is alive and pumping today. It's not making me a lot of money these days, and I don't spend much time or effort maintaining it, but it's still churning away. It was a tremendous little business that I built that's taught me the power of building an online business on Paid Search. And it's universal. It works for virtually every industry and profession, which is why I'm now a strategic direct response consultant. I know the value of working with someone who's done it, who knows what works and what doesn't, and understands the critical emotional component. That's what I'm now sharing with you.

The Inside Baseball on Building a Direct Response Campaign

So let me walk you through how I build marketing programs today. This is going to be a little inside baseball because I'm in the business of sharing my knowledge and helping companies in a wide range of service industries and professional practices to make more money using online direct response marketing. You are one of my markets.

But just as I learned early on from Ryan Deiss, I have some homework to do before I can move ahead with my plans for a marketing campaign. I need to narrow my focus, calculate the business metrics and build a profile of my market that identifies that market's wants and needs, fears and concerns. So let's take it from the top.

Niche. You know me as a strategic consultant because that's the way I've presented myself throughout this book. But first and foremost, I'm a businessman experienced in building my own Emotional Direct Response Marketing campaigns. I can analyze markets and pinpoint the opportunities—just as I learned early on from Ryan Deiss.

I've spent years building my copywriting skills, having trained at the feet of some of marketing's best—Dan Kennedy, Bob Bly, John Carlton, Joe Sugarman, Clayton Makepeace, Gary Bencivenga, John Caples and John Carlton. Google any of their names and you'll see the respect they carry among their peers. I've earned my stripes, having spent ten's of 1,000s of dollars in studying and countless hours in doing.

I also know how to put together a winning Google AdWords PPC campaign. And earned my living doing exactly that for many years. I can analyze and bid on keywords with the best of them and have worked with Google long enough to have mastered the subtleties of using long-tail keywords and GeoLocation to narrow a search and optimize my results. I always get the greatest bang for the buck—spending the least amount of money while putting my ads in front of the people most likely to want to buy what I have to sell.

As I proved with my hypnosis products, there's a market for practically anything. But as I've studied market opportunities, I've become increasingly interested in working with service businesses, professional practices and physicians. That's my sweet spot.

While I have outlined on my skills and interests, I still have to settle on a niche that's narrow enough to keep my copywriting and AdWord buys focused for maximum success. A website that includes everything I've just listed will be a worthless brochure site, about as interesting and inspiring as a cup of tepid tea in a snowstorm. But through my research and observations of the medical practices here in South Florida, I finally find my niche. My real business opportunity is as an Emotional Direct Response strategic consultant—working with physicians; hiring and directing writers, designers, and AdWords pros; and coordinating all the moving parts that constitute a direct response campaign. And the medical specialty where I believe I can do the greatest good is plastic surgery.

Business Metrics. With niche in hand, I have three sets of metrics to analyze:

1. What I need to charge to make the business viable. It has to be affordable, but it must be enough to run the business profitably, pay my staff and support my family and me.

2. What plastic surgeons make, and how much additional revenue a direct response campaign could bring in.

3. What is the size of the market for plastic surgery in my geographic location.

Armed with all this, I can set my rates, calculate the lifetime value of a plastic surgeon and determine just how much I can afford to spend to get a new client. If I don't make enough per client to pay for my marketing, I can't make it up in volume.

Market. With enough research I can create a demographic profile of plastic surgeons. But this still leaves me with questions: What do plastic surgeons want from their practice? What problems do they face achieving their goals? What's their Number One challenge? And what kinds of preconceptions do they have about marketing and advertising? Some psychographic observations will help. But when I turn to VALS, I begin to realize that plastic surgeons come in all shapes, sizes and personalities. They are Survivors, Sustainers, Belongers, Emulators, Achievers, I-Am-Me, Experientials, Socially Conscious and Integrateds.

Only when I consider the physician, rather than the person can I narrow my profile. These are surgeons. They are educated and skilled men and women...with a passion for surgery. And they strive for success. My plastic surgeons are Achievers. But what, besides running a successful, profitable practice, keeps them up at night?

I have an ace up my sleeve. I can go to the source and ask. Now there are several ways I can do this:

1. I can pump my plastic surgeon friends for answers. And I might try to do this, but I want to be careful not to become a pest. A few short, casual conversations shouldn't be too imposing.

2. I can make cold calls (telemarketing) to plastic surgeons and ask them if they are interested in booking an appointment for a free marketing consultation. While ostensibly I'd be selling an appointment to discuss marketing services, the real value to me will be information gathering. But outbound telemarketing interrupts a physician's busy day, and I know it will be hard to get physicians on the phone.

3. I can send a direct mail piece in the form of a survey with a few questions about their business goals and concerns. It's

99

more expensive. Even though I can do the copywriting, I still have design, printing and postage costs. But my business metrics indicate that I can afford to go ahead with this approach.

In addition to a few casual conversations—on the golf course and over lunch—I opt for Door Number Three. I don't expect a huge response, but with the right pitch and an intriguing Call to Action (to receive 6 practice-building strategies tailored for plastic surgeons in the lucrative, but crowded, South Florida market), I should get enough surveys back to answer my questions. Plus, it puts my name in front of a lot of local plastic surgeons who might later respond to my campaign. The survey serves as my first "touch."

Message. Once I have a sense of plastic surgeons' issues, I can craft my message using all the techniques we've been discussing about Emotional Direct Response copy. I make it about the surgeon's wants and pain points. I won't be writing about Marc Savage...not yet. While I can talk about building a practice and making more money, I've learned that plastic surgeons want to do more surgeries. Botox may yield higher lifetime-value patients, and some may opt for that niche, but deep down it's surgery they love and spent so many years training to do.

So what if I could show plastic surgeons a way to make more money doing what they love? Ah, now that just might resonate. So I have my headline: "How Any Plastic Surgeon Can Quickly Add at Least 3 MEGA-Profitable Surgeries a Month—Every Month—with Autopilot Consistency." Do I have your attention? That's a lot more compelling than "I'm Marc Savage. Call Me and I'll Share My Secrets of Emotional Direct Response Marketing." The body copy will deliver on the promise of my headline by building even greater emotional connection, answering questions, showing that I know what plastic surgeons want, and creating a desire to work with me.

Call to Action. I need a kick-ass Call to Action. I choose to do a free report, which I call "7 Secret Business-Building Tips You'll Never Get from Your Accountant." To get a copy, physicians call a toll-free number and leave a name and number. That's it. They don't have to talk with anyone, which frees up my staff and doesn't make the callers feel they are about to be strong-armed into a meeting. Someone on my staff calls to confirm and get the address, and the report is mailed.

The report provides useful content, but it's also a sales tool designed to move a prospective physician to a phone consultation. This will be our first conversation, and it's an opportunity for the surgeon to learn more about my strategy and ask questions. Basically we're determining if we're a good fit to work together, and if the answer is yes, we schedule a second meeting (either by phone again or face-to-face). At that time, I will present a proposal for a solution and disclose my fees. The plastic surgeon is buying from that final presentation and proposal. And with check in hand, I get to work.

While I always recommend automating as much of the pre-sell process as possible, how much is dependent on market preferences and the amount of money the service will cost. In this case, I decide that plastic surgeons warrant a lot of hands-on attention from me.

Media. While we've been talking about the advantages of using Google AdWords Pay Per Click advertising, the market is going to determine the best media choice. And in this case it's not on the Internet. Let me explain why. Until you started reading this book, I'm betting that you didn't know much about AdWords or Emotional Direct Response Marketing, and even if you do, you probably never imagined it to be something you can use effectively. If your market doesn't know that a solution exists, they're never going to search it. Paid Search is the wrong media to reach plastic surgeons about marketing. It's a good thing I focused on my market before choosing my media. Buying keywords and writing search ads would be a costly waste of my time and money.

Instead I opt for direct mail, and specifically a postcard with my headline, emotional copy and Call to Action all clearly laid out. This is more expensive than AdWords because of the design, printing and postage, but it's the best media for the job. The postcard sells the phone call to get the free report. And from the phone call, I'm up-selling the plastic surgeon to a solution (consultation) that includes the price—all for 30 minutes to an hour of our time. I will explain the costs and my prices, which are going to run $10,000 to $15,000 for the initial consultation, building a typical niche website and setting up the AdWords program. Sending some traffic to the website may be $1,500 to $3,000 a month with me managing the traffic. You can get traffic for less than $1,500, but it's me managing the traffic to make sure it's working and delivering quality leads. That's important because good management and tracking will increase conversions and actually lower the overall cost per lead—the savings are in the efficiencies and quality of traffic that turns into more leads. I'm selling an Emotional Direct Response Marketing campaign optimized for success.

A Few Tips and Reminders

As I explained at the outset of this chapter, I'm not delving into the technical aspects of building a website. Teaching you to write HTML code, the differences between Pages and Posts in WordPress, and showing you how to design an attractive, inviting website is beyond the scope of this book. It's also not something you should waste your time trying to learn. You don't need to know how to build the navigation across pages, but you do need to know the basics. An Emotional Direct Response website has five pages—a landing page (homepage) and four support pages:

- **Landing Page (Homepage)**—This is where your headline and long-form sales copy go. And don't forget to include your Call to Action on this and every page. You'll make your promise and deliver on that promise by anticipating a prospective patient's questions. This is a strong emotional sell; the other four pages are your supporting evidence.

- **About Us**—This is your chance to talk about you and your practice. Keep most of the focus on the physicians as people do business with other people...not their companies or surgical centers. Include your Call to Action.

- **FAQ**—Answer only the most commonly asked questions that you haven't covered in the sales letter. Experience will tell you what people most want to know. Don't try to be exhaustive. The FAQs are the questions that just keep popping up during phone calls and consults. Yes, the Call to Action needs to appear here, too.

- **Before-and-After Pictures**—This page is particularly important for promoting your procedure or treatment. People want to see results and imagine how great they're going to look. Don't forget your Call to Action.

- **Testimonials**—You can come up with a better name...like "Satisfied Patients" or "Beautiful Breast Gallery." If you can get video or audio recordings, use them along with text. Remember to add the Call to Action.

I'll close this chapter by giving you one more tool that will help ensure your website sends the right message, in the right order, to prospective patients. That tool is an acronym: **AIDA**. It stands for Attention, Interest, Desire and Action. And really all your marketing should follow AIDA—not just your website—because it can help build the emotional response to a resounding crescendo of activity. Let me take you through each step:

A-Attention: Your headline grabs the Attention, and since about 80 percent of readers fail to get past the headline, you need to consider the headline to be 80 percent of your ad. In other words, 80 percent of your success is determined by that headline. No pressure here! You can't afford to throw it away or get the message wrong. It's why I might write 50 to 100 headlines for a campaign, sometimes more...just to get one, good attention-grabber. I keep a swipe file of the best headlines ever written by the best copywriters, and this serves as a good starting point to help stimulate the flow of ideas.

I-Interest: Now, a good headline can also create Interest. It can get your prospective patient's attention by asking an interesting, provocative question. "Are You Dissatisfied with Your Breasts?" That's possibly a great headline because if she says, "Yes," you'll get her interested in what you can offer that might give her greater satisfaction. Now, I'm not recommending that you try to work both Attention and Interest into the headline because it's much harder headline to write. But a good copywriter can do it. An easier way to do this is to write a sub-headline, which appears under the headline in a slightly smaller font size. Here's an example I might write for Tom:

HEADLINE: Thinning Hair Have You Afraid?

SUB-HEADLINE: You Have a Lot Less to Fear than You Think!

The question will get Tom's attention. After all, he has several fears: fear of looking older than his years, fear that women won't find him attractive, fear that he might look too old to get ahead in his job, and fear about the cost and pain associated with hair transplantation. The sub-head should get Tom's interest because maybe he doesn't have as much to fear as he thought. With interest piqued, he will probably stay around to read the sales letter. In fact, the sub-head sets up the sales letter to build even greater interest.

D-Desire: And speaking of the sales letter, this is where you do more than continue building Interest. The sales letter (or body copy) is where you build Desire. Here's how the progression works:

HEADLINE: "Are You Happy with Your Breasts?" (Attention. Interest.)

SUB-HEADLINE: "If you're like most of my patients, you're dreaming of a fuller figure." (Interest.)

Now, if they are happy with their breasts, it doesn't matter. They move on. And, of course, since we'll set your AdWords campaign up right, you'll only get clickthroughs from women who are unhappy. The implication in the sub-head is that you are going to solve their problem. They will read on.

BODY COPY: "Many of my patients come to me because they just had a baby and they need a Mommy Makeover. Their breasts have lost their firm, pre-baby perkiness. Life is taking its toll. Some of my patients feel they are too small to look dazzling in a bikini. They've wanted bigger breasts their whole adult lives. And a few are afraid their husbands are looking a little too intently at other women. I understand that looking your best is important both to how you feel about yourself and how you want others to see you..."

These are all valid concerns that women share with their plastic surgeons, and I'm sure you've heard many more. I'm just throwing out a few of these to show you how we write body copy that begins to deliver on the promise in the headline and build Desire throughout the sales letter. You're building a story that intensifies Desire by validating a prospective patient's issues, sharing stories about how you resolved even worse issues that other women faced, and showing how you can help. Your Testimonial page and the Before-and-After pictures will further add to Desire. Here's what Jill H. has to say about putting the embarrassment of buying a 32-A bra behind her forever. Testimonials play to Desire: "If Dr. Jones could do that for them, she can do that for me. Oh, my God, I have to call this doctor today. I'm ready to take the next step."

A-Action: What is the next step? It's not scheduling surgery. That's not what your Desire should be building to...not yet. And that's not what you're selling in your Call to Action. But it could be picking up the phone and calling for more information, or downloading a free report. Whatever it is, Desire should lead your prospect to take Action. Your Call to Action gives a person the option to take whatever Action you want to be the next step...call, take the free information, or do nothing. Remember, doing nothing is always an option, especially when life is calling: "My child's crying in the background. I have to get my child." Or, "I'll have to look at this later because right now I'm late for my meeting with the boss."

To keep the Desire building just a little bit longer and get Sarah or Tom to take action, you need what's called an irresistible offer. The typical offer is call for your free consult. But what's irresistible about that? Everybody offers it, and so what? But even if everybody didn't offer it, there's nothing really all that great about a free consult. It's boring. But if your Call to Action is a free "How to Get Your Most Beautiful Breasts Strategy Session," that's not quite as boring. I don't love it and would want to spend time fine-tuning and tweaking the final version, but without doing a thing it blows away a call for a free consult. While your offer is still the same as everyone else's, what you call it can make a big difference. Even the smallest element of your Emotional Direct Response campaign needs to be carefully considered and optimized for great results.

But that's how you can use AIDA to create copy for your site. We haven't built the site, but by working through MARKET, MESSAGE and MEDIA, we have created some pretty solid bone structure. You're ready to start working on the AdWords PPC campaign that's going to drive traffic to your new, niche, optimized website.

Chapter 4
Get Traffic Fast!
The Media of Immediacy!

"You use Google to test everything and get the message right—and then you go to the other places."

– Perry Marshall, online marketing strategist

In the Preface, I wrote that this book is to help you get your message in front of the people most actively seeking your services as a plastic surgeon. We've built our Emotional Direct Response campaign around the three-prong strategy of Market – Message – Media, and at this point, we've worked through the Market and Message components by:

1. Selecting a niche procedure or treatment for your direct response campaign,

2. Understanding the lifetime value of a patient,

3. Identifying your ideal market, and

4. Building a website and writing emotionally compelling copy that draws prospective patients to want to connect with you and take the next step—starting with responding to your Call to Action.

But even the most focused website and professionally written copy cannot deliver patients without your ability to reach men and women who want and are actively looking for the services you have to offer. In other words, you need to attract highly targeted traffic to your website—people who are ready to buy. We've touched briefly upon traffic and Google AdWords Paid Search in previous chapters. Now it's time to go in depth. It's time to bring your marketing campaign together.

In an Internet environment comprised of nearly one billion websites, some 250 million blogs, and billions of users communicating on the popular social media sites, getting found and engaging the interest of readers is no small feat...at least not without a strategy built to optimize your success. While ecommerce is growing at a rate of about 10 percent annually and worldwide use of the Internet has never been stronger and more pervasive, getting found in a sea of churning content requires 1) control for the short-term strategy and 2) persistence for the medium- and long-term strategies.

While I'm going to show you how short-, medium- and long-term strategies can work together to deliver results, your immediate focus needs to be on the short term. It only makes sense that after you've invested in the development of a niche website, emotional copywriting and the creation of a Call to Action that converts prospects into patients (collectively, these comprise your marketing piece), you need quick results. In times past, you might have created a direct mail letter, brochure, flyer, postcard, or even hired a telemarketer, and bought lists of prospective patients in your area. Today, the Internet replaces the prospect list. And unlike traditional direct mail (outbound), you're connecting with people who are already searching for what you have to offer. It's called Inbound Marketing, and it's important because prospective patients self-select when they make the first step to choose you by clicking on your text ad. Inbound marketing is efficient. It's less intrusive. And it's cost-effective. Generally, inbound leads cost about 60 percent less than outbound leads.

Media 101: A Quick Overview

If you read much about Internet marketing, you may have seen references to Owned – Earned – Paid media. These are the three basic types of media and traffic available through the Internet. Here's a simple description of each:

Owned: In terms of its place in your marketing strategy, think branding and advertising. Owned media is the wide range of content you create and post across the many Internet platforms, and much of it is free, requiring only the investment of your time and creativity. Examples of owned media include social postings, website development, blog postings, webinar events, digital press releases, comments on forums, articles, and audio and video recordings. Technically, even your niche website is an example of owned media. While owned media is a good way to build a following and attract prospects, it is not a strategy that works quickly; it requires months, even years of development. You also don't have the advantage of being able to narrow your audience only to prospects who are ready to buy. <u>This is a medium- to long-term strategy that when well done and added to regularly can scale...in time.</u>

Earned: Think Grumpy Cat—the Snowshoe Siamese with the perpetual frown whose photo posted to Reddit went viral. Within six months, the cat had a Facebook Page with millions of Likes, her face on the cover of national magazines, and dozens of toy and food deals, including Friskies cat food. Earned media can take you from $0 to five- and six-figure income in a matter of months. But fame is elusive, and no one seems able to manufacture viral success with any reliability. Earned media can come from content in the form of posts, videos, photos, audio—anything that can be put up on the Internet. If it captures the imagination of Internet audiences, fame spreads quickly through word of mouth, sharing, and the buzz of commentary from others. Go viral and you'll have success, but <u>with so little control over the odds, it is best to only *hope* for an earned status but not waste time and effort trying to achieve it.</u>

Paid: Think traditional classified ads running in the newspaper, direct mail packages sent to your home or business, advertorials (often referred to as native content), and infomercials. Paid media in their digital forms are the banner ads and display ads running on commercial and media websites, pop-up ads, the ads embedded in YouTube videos, and most

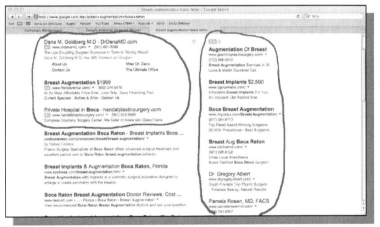

important to us, Paid Search (also referred to as Pay Per Click or PPC) ads like Google AdWords and Bing Ads that show up in Search. As the name suggests, there are fees associated with Paid media, but the response can be very quick and highly rewarding. It's a pay-to-play strategy. <u>Paid is the short-term strategy that delivers the best and most immediate results because you can put</u>

these ads in front of the people most likely to buy. And when you find a formula of keywords, ad copy and locations that work, it's the easiest to scale (grow).

The screenshot above is from a Google search for "breast augmentation boca raton." I've circled the Paid Search ads. Note how they wrap around the (non-paid) organic results.

The Ubiquity of Paid Search

If you're one of the people who almost always leapfrogs the PPC ads that appear every time you run a Google or Bing search, then you might be thinking, *well, doesn't everybody?* You're about to be surprised. I've quoted before from the Hanapin Marketing report, *The State of Paid Search*, but their findings deserve more of our attention. The survey targeted account specialists and executives/managers in companies that could afford to use just about any marketing or advertising media they wanted. Fully 63 percent of respondents have PPC budgets of $300,000 or more annually.

But don't let the size of their budgets discourage you. Yes, you could easily spend that kind of money on Paid Search, but you don't have to. You can (in fact you should) start small as you polish and fine-tune your tactics. You can spend as little as $5 or $10 a day if you want. My reason for sharing the results of the Hanapin Marketing study is that they queried some of the most savvy marketers making decisions today, and here's what they found:

- 95 percent consider text ads (Paid Search) "important/very important" and 64 percent deem remarketing "important/very important." (I'll explain remarketing later in this chapter.)

112

- At the same time, 68 percent of respondents consider ads on social media sites "moderate-to-not important." They're not impressed with the ROI.

- 72 percent of companies will have a higher ad spend this year than last year.

- 73 percent are focusing their Paid Search strategy on Google AdWords.

    Businesses use Paid Search because:

1. Anywhere from 73 percent to 90 percent (depending on the report you read) of consumers and business buyers start their buying process with Search. So if you want to be part of the buying equation, you need to be on the first page of virtually every buyer search that queries for what you are selling.

2. Paid Search is the easiest, most reliable and most sustainable way to ensure your ad appears on the first page of a search query. Using SEO strategies with organic (non-Paid) search is a distant and unreliable second. This is a critical point. According to Chitika Insights, its sample study of more than 8 million queries found that only 6 percent of users clicked through to the second page of a search. You have to be on page one to be seen.

3. Companies with highly optimized ad campaigns that include carefully selected keywords and ongoing tracking and measurement are getting results. And according to a September 2013 report from MarketLive, while organic search results outperform Paid Search and receive more clicks, the revenue generated from each (conversion of click into an action that leads to a next step) is very close. Retail, organic search accounted for 27 percent of revenue, while Paid Search delivered 21 percent of revenue. Not bad for a

media option that many people think is ignored; <u>the key is to develop good, engaging ads</u>.

So what's the bottom line? The best marketers will create a strategy that includes Paid and Owned media, but they will stake their initial efforts on Paid, which gives them more control and a greater opportunity to get their ad on the first page of a search query...where it can be seen. And they will optimize their ad (and the keywords and metrics behind it) with the same care and attention to the wants and needs of their target markets that went into creating a niche website and writing copy that connects with prospects.

Why Google AdWords?

For the explanation of Paid Search that follows, I am going to limit my screenshots and examples to Google AdWords. While the concepts I'm presenting will generally work the same across all search engine platforms (e.g., Bing, Yahoo!, Ask, AOL, etc.), Google AdWords is by far the largest player. Google still commands about 70 percent market share for the placement of text ads, and at least that percentage of end-user searches also start on Google. There's a reason we say, "I'm going to Google that," when we want to run a search. Bing is growing and slowly gaining on Google, but it has a long way to go to catch the industry leader.

While I will walk you through the basic elements of a well-optimized Google AdWords ad, I need to warn you that my presentation is far from comprehensive. The art and science that go into developing a successful Pay Per Click campaign require more space than I can allot to them here. And I've done this deliberately.

First, my goal is to give you an overall strategy for online success built on the Emotional Direct Response Marketing model. This little book is designed to help you understand what works, and why.

And **second**, in terms of the necessary basic steps, while Google AdWords is fairly easy and intuitive, creating a *successful* ad that attracts highly receptive traffic is another matter. It's one more reason I always recommend that you work with a seasoned professional strategist. As a plastic surgeon, your attention is best kept focused on your medical practice, not the intricacies of a marketing campaign. Just as I would only want to trust some part of my anatomy to an experienced plastic surgeon, so too you need to put your marketing in the hands of an experienced Emotional Direct Response Marketing strategist. <u>There is money to be made with Google AdWords, but there is also money to be lost— if you don't know what you're doing</u>.

That said, if you are determined to learn how to run your own Emotional Direct Response Marketing campaign, I still recommend that you start out working with a professional. It's the fastest way to see results. Learn from a pro, read several of the many tutorial books on AdWords and Pay Per Click available, and only gradually take over the process. Here are a few places to start: *Ultimate Guide to Google AdWords* by Perry Marshall and Bryan Todd, *Advanced Google AdWords, Second Edition* by Brad Geddes, and *Google AdWords for Dummies* by Howie Jacobs.

Let's dig in.

Key Components of a Google AdWords Campaign

If you don't already have one, you need to begin by creating a Google account. A simple, free Gmail (Google email) or Google+ account is all you need to establish yourself on Google. To enter the AdWords site, click on the word Advertising in the bottom-left corner of the Google.com page. You'll be taken to the instructional section where you can learn all about the many ways you can advertise through Google. You'll find articles and videos that will explain how to create and post your first ad. On first blush, the breadth and depth of their information can be overwhelming—there are that many options and components for advanced Paid Search marketers to consider.

Once you have an account, you can go straight to AdWords by typing adwords.google.com. After you sign in, you'll see the dashboard.

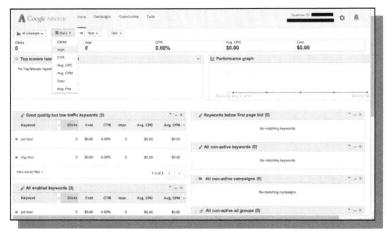

Now, before we go any farther, I need to warn you that AdWords is not without several serious pitfalls that can cost you a lot more than you'll ever earn. As Jason McDonald, author of *Google AdWords Gotchas*, warns, "Friends don't let friends drive drunk, and friends don't let friends use Google AdWords without a basic understanding of the four 'gotchas' that can cost a lot of money." In truth, there are many more, and in his 2014 edition, McDonald includes five gotchas. They include: understanding how to use "match types" with keywords, using the Display Network, expanding your reach through enhanced campaigns, writing great ad copy, and using AdWords in conjunction with SEO (search engine optimization) and social media—what I call the medium- and long-term strategies.

To make my point that knowing what you're doing is critical, let me share a true story from a client who decided to go it alone before turning to me for help. This client is in a non-medical service business, and he wanted to use AdWords to reach highly qualified traffic and boost sales. He has an office manager who is smart, very conscientious and whom he trusts implicitly. So he asked her to take charge of setting up his AdWords account. I mean, how hard could it be? Everyone's doing it! Right? Well, she was able to set up the account, write a small ad, select a few keywords and link his credit card to the account so he could pay for every click he received. And it didn't take long for the results to come. The ad received plenty of clicks—enough to burn through $14,000 of charges to his credit card—without a single new customer. His first question to me: "What went wrong?"

I told him, and I'll share the reasons with you now. Here are four of the biggest, most common mistakes newbie advertisers make:

1. Failure to select keywords that target people *ready to buy*.

2. Disconnect between the ad and the website. She got the clicks but the website copy wasn't converting clicks into customers.

3. Failure to put a limit on how much Google could charge to the credit card each day. The clicks just kept coming, running up the credit card.

4. Failure to test and measure the campaign results on an hourly, daily or even weekly schedule in order to figure out what was working and what wasn't. We call this process of testing, tracking and fine-tuning "running the analytics," and it's critical to success.

Here's the problem: For all Google's ability to give you information on how to create a campaign, there's so much to know it'll leave your head swimming with options, techniques and enough jargon and specialized terminology to choke a horse.

To create a new ad campaign, select "Campaign" from the menu at the top of the screen. Then click on the red button "+ Campaign" and from the drop-down menu, select "Search Network only."

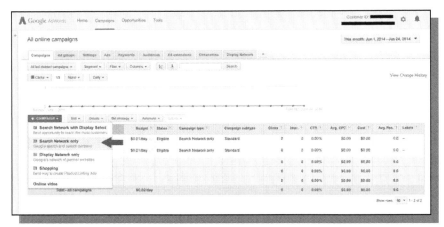

You'll then need to name your Campaign and set your Max Bid and daily ad spend (budget). Start very small, say $1; you can always go back and change the numbers later.

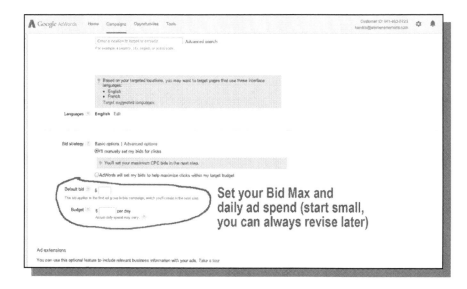

Set your Bid Max and daily ad spend (start small, you can always revise later)

There are a lot of moving parts to a campaign; I'm going to share with you four lessons and take you through these basics:

- Selecting Keywords

- Writing Text Ads

- Choosing Where Your Ads Will Run

- Running the Analytics

- Scaling Your Paid Search Campaign

Paid Search Terminology

Before we go too far, I need to introduce you to some of the Paid Search terms you'll need to know:

Bid: Since buying keywords is competitive, you must state the maximum amount you are willing to pay for a click on a keyword (Max Bid).

Clicks: The action of end-user searchers when they see an ad that captures their interest and want more information. Clicking on ads redirects searchers to advertisers' websites or landing pages.

Clickthrough Rate (CTR): A metric for calculating the success or failure of an ad by dividing the number of clicks by the number of impressions (times your ad appears).

Conversion Rate: A metric for calculating the success or failure of your ad to get the prospect to take the next step (Call to Action). It may be to download a report, call for information, book a consultation, etc. To measure the rate for converting traffic into leads, divide conversions by the number of clicks.

Cost Per Click (CPC): The amount of money advertisers actually pay for every ad click. This is

con't

---

may be the same as your Max Bid, but it can vary depending on how many people are competing for a keyword.

Display Network: Beyond ads that come up in search, Display Network is a collection of individual websites, blogs and videos (such as YouTube) where your Google AdWords ads can appear. Bing has a similar service called Content Network.

Geo-targeting: Target ads to your particular geographic region by adding a location to your keyword phrase, such as "Botox Injections NYC." Geo-targeting your keywords limits your ads to appear only in search results that for your location.

Google Analytics: Google's free service for tracking ad and website activity and collecting statistics on website visits. Useful when testing and optimizing your ad campaign.

Impressions: The number of times your ad displays—whether on search pages or the Display Network sites.

Keyword: A word or phrase that identifies the subject of your content and anticipates what prospects will query for in Search. A Long-tail keyword is a phrase of three or more words that help to narrow a search to better target your market. Long-tail keywords are typically less competitive and less expensive. Keywords are also an important part of Search Engine Optimization (SEO).

Pay Per Click (PPC): This is another name for Paid Search and Display Network ads.

Quality Score (QS): A search engine's algorithm used to set advertisers' keyword costs and position on a search page. It's determined based on the quality and relevance of an ad and landing page. The higher the Quality Score, the lower the cost of keywords and the higher the ad's position on a is

con't

search page.

Remarketing: A Display Network service that allows your ads to appear on selected websites within the Display Network, once an end user has viewed your website. Remarketed ads serve as reminders to revisit a website previously visited.

Return On Advertising Spend (ROAS): The amount earned in revenue per the amount spent on advertising.

Search Engine Optimization (SEO): The process of improving the position of organic (non-paid) search results by using a complex algorithm of keywords, high-quality content, and relevant landing pages.

Search Network: A collection of Google search sites (Google Maps, Search, Shopping, Images and Groups) and non-Google partner search sites (e.g., AOL) where you can run Paid Search ads.

Text Ad: A form of ad that is all text (no images or video) and includes a headline, two lines of descriptive copy and a URL link.

LESSON ONE—CAREFULLY SELECTED KEYWORDS MAKE YOUR CLICKS COUNT:
When a click doesn't convert, you're spending money without any ROI. You want your Paid Search ads to come up only when a prospective patient is searching for a plastic surgeon in your marketing niche. Furthermore, you want to target prospects ready to buy and who are within your geographic location. Not only is there no business among the wrong (untargeted) prospects, you're paying for every wrong click on your ad...whether it results in a patient or not.

Selecting Keywords

I suppose it's a little like the chicken or the egg conundrum as to whether you should write your ad first or select your keywords. Personally, I like to start with the keywords analysis because I try to include some of my keywords in the headline and text of my ads.

Selecting good keywords that convert and deliver traffic that's ready to purchase takes a little thought and experimentation. Google helps make your job easier by providing its Keyword Planner. Here you can enter possible keywords and keyword phrases to see monthly search volume; competition for keywords; a range of alternate, related keywords; and suggested bid prices. Prices for keywords will range from a few cents to $15 or $20, with prices based on bidding competition among AdWords advertisers. The more people competing for a keyword and their willingness to pay more for the top position among search results, the more a keyword will cost. Buying keywords is like bidding at an auction only in Google you have the option of automating or managing the process manually. In most cases, the advertiser who bids highest gets the top position on page one of Google.

Select the Keyword Planner from the Tools menu (at the top of the AdWords window), and when the first page appears (see image on the previous page), select the first option in order to start experimenting with possible keywords.

Next, fill out the top part of the form (don't worry about filters, negative keywords, targeting, etc. right now). The main

thing is to type in a few keywords you think you might want and see the results:

A note about keyword costs: You may be wondering how much is too much to pay for a keyword and how can you can keep your ad spend under control. Here are a few pointers:

1. I suppose the simple answer is that with experimentation you'll figure out how much you can afford to pay and get a good return on your investment. It's not unlike the process you went through to determine the lifetime value of your patients. Of course, given the cost of most plastic surgery procedures, you can afford to pay $15 or even $20 for a keyword that puts your ad in front of a select group of prospective patients who are ready to buy—*assuming you are getting new patients from your AdWords campaign.*

   But here's my caveat: It takes some testing and tracking to determine which of the keywords you select are giving you the best results, the most conversions and the greatest number of new patients. Until you've determined that your ad, keywords, website, and Call to Action are fully optimized to deliver patients, you need to move ahead slowly.

2. The best protection is to make sure you set a maximum daily ad spend that you can afford. Again, once you are confident of your results, you can begin to scale your campaign and raise the limit of your maximum daily ad spend. At the height of my Paid Search business. I was spending $20,000 a month, but I also was bringing in about twice that amount in sales.

3. Finally, Google uses a formula to set the minimum cost you will pay for a keyword click and the position on the page when your ad appears:

Max Bid X Quality Score = Ad Rank

Ad Rank of Next Bidder / Your Quality Score + $0.01 =
Actual CPC Price

Bidder	Max Bid	x Quality Score	= Ad Rank (Highest gets top position)	Actual Cost Per Click (Price)
Advertiser A	$5	10	50	32/10 + $0.01 = $3.21
Advertiser B	$8	4	32	22/4 + $0.01 = $5.51
Advertiser C	$11	2	22	Highest Price Paid

The first thing you need to understand is the power of the right keywords to 1) deliver the best possible prospects—people ready to select the procedure or treatment you are promoting—and 2) help keep your costs under control. I'll use the Botox treatments niche market to explain what I mean. If you've developed a website and a message to sell your Botox treatments, you want to focus your keywords around that niche. The keyword "plastic surgeon," for example, potentially will place your text ad in front of everyone from California to Maine who is interested in plastic surgery. And that includes women looking for breast augmentation, men wanting a hair transplant, anyone interested in rhinoplasty, and everyone who might have a question about plastic surgery.

So "Botox" or "Botox Treatment" will definitely be better keyword options. Better...but still not good enough. People often begin using online search to gather information weeks and even months before they are ready to consider buying. Someone who goes to Google and types in the search query "Botox" may only want to know something about Botox. Take Jane; her best friend's mother just had a Botox treatment, and Jane is curious to know more about the treatment. Jane's not a prospective patient.

But if she clicks on your ad to learn more, you still pay for the click.

Similarly, Rihanna is a 40-year-old office worker. She might be a viable prospect at some time in the future, but right now she's just collecting information about Botox: What's the active ingredient in Botox? How much do treatments typically cost? How often would she need follow-up treatments? What happens if she doesn't continue to get periodic treatments once she starts? Rihanna is in the very early stages of investigation; she's not nearly ready to select a physician. But again, if your ad comes up when she searches on "Botox," and if she clicks on it, you pay for the click but you won't get a new patient.

And finally, there's Maureen. She's 52 and hates the small lines forming above her upper lip. She's ready to find a plastic surgeon that can administer Botox. She goes to Google and enters "Botox," and just as you hoped, your ad appears on the first page of search results. Maureen likes your ad and clicks through to your website. So far so good. She reads your copy, looks at your testimonials, and likes the before-and-after pictures so much that she takes advantage of your Call to Action to get your free report, *Beautiful Botox Basics*. And then she notices that your offices are in Boca Raton. But Maureen lives in Southern California. You just paid for her click and delivered a terrific free report that will help Maureen move forward with her plans, but she'll be looking for another physician—someone closer to her home.

Keywords need to be as specific as possible: 1) as close to what prospective patients are searching on when they are ready to buy, and 2) geo-targeted to your location. "Botox" and "Botox Treatment" are informational words...NOT buy words. There are two basic categories of keywords:

- **Short tail:** These are the simplest and shortest keywords. "Botox" and "Botox Treatment" are examples of short-tail keywords. Your ads will get more impressions, meaning they will come up in more searches, but the audience will include everyone who wants to know anything about Botox, regardless of where they live and whether or not they are ready to purchase your treatment. My recent test, using Google Keyword Planner on the keyword "Botox," showed an average of 246,000 monthly searches with a suggested bid price of $5.75 per click. Now we'll compare that with some long-tail results.

• **Long tail:** Author and former editor-in-chief of *Wired* magazine, Chris Anderson, popularized the term "long tail." He refers to the retailing strategy where you sell a few each of a lot of items over a very long time, as opposed to selling a lot of a few popular (trendy) items in a short time. The long-tail strategy usually wins.

In your Paid Search keyword strategy, you are looking for keyword phrases that are specific to your niche and will target fewer people more precisely within the group of people most likely to purchase a particular treatment or procedure from you. "Affordable Botox Injection Treatment Boca Raton" is an example of a six-word, long-tail keyword. So is "Best Botox Physician Boca Raton FL." Long-tail keywords are typically phrases of three words or more, and on average five to six words. They have the advantage of limited ad impressions to people most likely to want what you are selling and—in most cases—of being less competitive (fewer people bidding on them) and less expensive to buy.

To give you a comparison, I took two simple long-tail keywords, "Botox Injections Boca Raton" and "Botox Boca Raton," to see how they compare with the short-tail keyword "Botox Injections." You can refer back to the screenshot on page 114. The short-tail keyword "Botox Injections" receives an average of 8,100 monthly searches (many fewer than the 246,000 of "Botox") and has a suggested bid price of $6.91, which is higher than the $5.75 bid price for "Botox" (clearly there is more competition for "Botox Injections"). "Botox Injections" may be more of a buy word than "Botox," but you really want a keyword that geo-targets your location. When I entered "Botox Injections Boca Raton," I found no results, which doesn't mean it's a bad keyword, only that not enough people are using it to provide a significant statistical measure or set a minimum bid price. And when I did a Google search on that same keyword, I found more than 75,000 organic search results and several text ads geo-targeted for the Boca Raton area. I can probably pick up that keyword cheap; it certainly deserves testing.

Finally, I put "Botox Boca Raton" into the Keyword Planner and received the results I was looking for: an average of 90 monthly searches and the suggested bid price is $8.84. It's more competitive, and will cost a little more because you're up against some savvy AdWords marketers, but it's promising. Very promising.

Understanding the Value of Long-Tail Keywords

On first look, long-tail keywords may not seem like the best opportunity for getting traffic. The main reason being that you're going to get fewer impressions and most likely fewer clicks. So let's think about this for a minute. More of the wrong people clicking who are not ready buy or who don't live near your practice is a waste of your money. *You want conversions. You want new patients.* Even if just 90 people search on your long-tail keyword each month and 45 percent click on your ad, that's 40 people who come to your

con't

website...every month!

If the focus and quality of your website converts 65 percent to act on your Call to Action, that's 26 people. And if 80 percent of those people read your report and want to move forward and become your patient, that's 21 people spending roughly $100 on their first Botox treatment. You'd bring in around $2100 for the month. Even at $8.84 per click, your AdWords campaign would cost you only $353.60 a month ($8.84 x 40 clicks).

Now, compare that with the short-tail keyword "Botox Injections." Of 8,100 people searching that keyword, if just 10 percent find your ad appropriate to their needs, that's 810 clicks. But if most are not interested in buying Botox, or are not yet ready, you might get just 3 percent who decide to opt-in on your Call to Action, which equals 24 people. And if 3 percent of them go forward and contact your office for a consultation, that's roughly 1 person a month. But at $6.91 per click, your monthly AdWords bill will be $5,597.10 ($6.91 x 810 clicks). You might break even if you were marketing breast augmentations, but selling Botox treatments, you'll lose money.

The difference between these projected long-tail and short-tail results are not unreasonable. Long-tail keywords reach a smaller number of people up front. But if they are buyers, it's a market with a much higher probability of converting.

Finally, I'll close this lesson on selecting keywords that count with two more tips:

1. If you decide to create several ads in the same niche, you want to set up your campaign so that you're not bidding against yourself for a keyword you want to use in multiple ad, inadvertently pushing up the bid price. By creating an Ad

Group, you select and bid on keywords once, and they apply to every ad in the Ad Group.

2. Consider competitive products when picking your keywords. In the case of Botox, there's a competitive product called Dysport. People close to making a buying decision may be comparing alternative treatments. You could create an ad that drives prospective patients to your website to get a free report that discusses the differences. If you get a lot of phone calls with questions about Dysport versus Botox, a special report could be just the thing to help you automate the marketing process and increase the number of informed prospects who call for a consultation. In that case, you'll probably increase your conversion rate. A long-tail keyword like "Botox versus Dysport Treatments Boca Raton" or "Differences Between Botox and Dysport Injections Miami" might be worth trying. And this brings us back to the question I posed in Chapter 2, *What are you selling?*

> *LESSON TWO—MAINTAIN A CLEAR FOCUS ON WHAT YOU'RE SELLING WHEN WRITING AD COPY: As we've discussed, an ad and a website won't sell an $8,000 procedure. Know what you're really selling and focus on what it'll take to get qualified prospects to take the next step. Look to your web copy and your Call to Action, and try writing an ad that promises what your website is set up to deliver. Lose sight of what you're selling, and you may get the clicks, but you won't get conversions.*

Writing Text Ads

While I like to work on my keywords first, if the copy on your website is fresh in your mind, you might want to start developing your AdWords campaign by writing a first draft of your ad copy.

You can edit, change and tweak your copy as often as you want as you're developing your campaign. For that matter, you can continue tweaking even after your campaign goes live. So relax and focus.

But before you start writing, spend a few minutes looking at some of the Google AdWords text ads created by other plastic surgeons. Try searching on "Dental Implants New York" or "Breast Augmentation Surgeon in Miami FL" or simply "Breast Augmentation."

In particular, study the ads in your niche market. Just as with our early look at websites and Yellow Page ads, you won't find a lot to imitate or many ideas to squirrel away in your copywriting swipe file. It's bad copywriting for all the usual reasons and more examples of incestuous marketing, but you'll at least get a sense for the elements that comprise an AdWords ad and how they look on the screen.

Take a look at the headlines, and you're going to see all the same problems that come up in most website headlines. There's no emotional connection, and the emphasis is typically on the physician or the surgical center. A few of the worst headlines that jumped out at me include: "Dr. John Doe," "Plastic Surgery Clinic," and "Award Winning Surgery." They're generic—with no mention of a niche. They appeal to the ego of the surgeon, not the wants, needs and concerns of the prospective patient. And they all look alike.

Why People Don't Click on Ads

Actually, we know that people do click on Paid Search ads. The proof is in the revenue good marketers are making.

con't

But I have a theory as to why so many people claim they don't click on ads. It's the ads themselves. They are so poorly conceived and badly written that no one is interested in clicking to learn more. And I don't blame them.

Think about your own browsing habits. You look at the ads, even if it's just a quick glance. If you see something you really want, you'll click. It's just that the preponderance of bad ads makes that such a rare occurrence that you too may claim that you never click on ads. I know that I look. And when I do click, it's because the advertiser knows how to capture my interest.

We've already spent a lot of time discussing Emotional Direct Response copywriting, so I'm going to limit myself here to the specific parameters you need to follow when writing a Google text ad and give you a list of do's and don'ts.

First the parameters. Text ads must:

- Be short and to the point.

- Include a Headline (25 characters maximum).

- Include two lines of Description Copy (35 characters maximum for each line).

- Include your URL.

The Display URL (the one shown in the ad) is also restricted to 35 characters, including the actual domain name and the extension (e.g., BotoxBeautifulFace.com/get-report). You don't have to add the www. Extensions can be anything that you feel might provide further inducement to click, such as /call-today or /save-now or /no-sag. If you want to use extensions, you'll need to create a URL that is short enough that the domain name plus extension together are no more than 35 characters. The Destination URL doesn't show in the ad, but it's the actual link to the page where a prospect is sent upon clicking.

If the landing page is your website's homepage, which is typical, your URLs might look like this.

Display URL: BotoxBeautifulFace.com/no-wrinkles (Everything to the right of the slant is fictitious and created for added interest.)

Destination URL: BotoxBeautifulFace.com (This is the actual link to your landing page.)

Text Ad Copywriting Tips, Techniques and Potential Mistakes

As you begin to write, you need to think about how you are going to get your message across in three short, compelling lines that define what you're selling and what your prospects want. Here are some things to consider (and try):

- Keep your name or the name of your practice out of the headline. Try to connect with your audience in your best Emotional Direct Response copywriting form.

- Keep your message specific to your niche.

- Set expectations with a promise that your website can deliver.

- Spend enough time working on your headline. This is the first place the eye goes. Make it stand out in a crowded field of mediocrity.

- Use a testimonial quote in your description or headline, such as: "I Love My New Look!!" or "Wow, I Just Lost 10 Years!"

- Ask a question that you know is important to prospective patients: Are You Ready for Botox? Want Quality Botox for Less? Feel self-conscious in a bikini?

- Make a story: "Friends said Sally looked tired. Now everyone wants her secret."

- Promote your Call to Action. If you have a special report or want phone calls, invite people to take the next step. "Hollywood secret for fresher face! Get your special report."

- Be careful about promoting your FREE report; it's an open invitation to information seekers and freebie hunters to click your link at your expense. Try SPECIAL report or Beautiful Breast Report or Natural Hair Forever. You want serious prospects.

- If you have a special offer, state it: "Your 1st Botox session ½ price."

- Give people your best benefit: "Look Younger Tomorrow" or "Grow Your Own Hair Again" or "Wear Your Bikini with Confidence."

- Include action words and active verbs that induce people to act and take the next step: "Click for Younger-Looking Skin."

- Include your location: Play to your local market and discourage people outside your region from clicking on your ad. You'll also do this with your keywords, but if you can be clever about how you work your location into the copy, go for it: "Vegas women have a skin secret" or "For Boca's own fountain of youth."

- Treat your description copy as two short sentences, and include punctuation. It makes reading easier.

- Create a Display URL that includes a keyword: YoungerFaceNow.com/botox-injections

- If you have a special offer that will entice prospects to click, promote it: ½ price month, membership discount program, a special report, questions answered, etc.

- Choose your words carefully. Avoid common, extra words without giving up readability, but avoid cryptic abbreviations.

LESSON THREE—FOR OPTIMAL RESULTS, THINK ABOUT ALL ELEMENTS OF YOUR CAMPAIGN: Your Emotional Direct Response Marketing campaign is only as good as the sum of its parts, and it's only as effective as its weakest link. For this reason, if any one component fails to perform, the entire campaign will fail to deliver qualified prospects that become patients.

It is because an Emotional Direct Response Marketing campaign is so dependent on every element performing that you must: 1) consider every possible way to get your ads in front of your target market and 2) optimize every element through testing, tracking, tweaking and testing some more.

Choosing Where Your Ads Will Run

To this point, I've been talking almost exclusively about Paid Search text ads triggered by keywords, but Google offers several other options experienced advertisers can use to reach their markets. While you always want to make Paid Search your primary AdWords venue, Google's Display Network and Retargeting Ads have a place as medium-term strategies.

Display Network. The Google Display Network opens up an array of opportunities for placing ads in front of targeted audiences on YouTube, Blogger, Gmail, mobile sites, and more than 2 million independent websites—reaching 90 percent of Internet users and serving up a total of more than 1 trillion impressions across the Network each month. You could scour the Internet and scan 100s of websites across the Internet looking for places that will take your ads, or you can let the Google Display Network do the heavy lifting and serve up sites targeted by category. It's convenient, and will get your ads on many top sites.

I still contend that Paid Search is your first and most expedient path to reaching your target market, but as your strategy matures and Paid Search begins to convert, you can increase your reach through the Display Network. Think of it as more similar to making a traditional media buy for a select set of magazines and/or newspapers—only it's all digital, and you have more control. Just as you might decide to run ads in beauty or health magazines, the Display Network let's you target digital media in the same categories.

The Display Network has two notable limitations, which is why this is a medium-term strategy: 1) rather than searching for information, users are going to these partner websites for the content. They are literally preoccupied with whatever article, application or video that took them to a site in the first place. So you're not going to have people's undivided attention. 2) because it's not Search, you can't target buyers exclusively. Here are a few ways to boost your chances for success:

- Post ONLY your most compelling and *proven* ads in the Display Network.

- In addition to your text ads, you can post video ads, image or banner ads, which may increase your chances of being seen.

- While you can choose to let Google select websites relevant for your ad, the manual option allows you to select specific websites by name and URL. Manual selection may be the better way to start small.

- To help you select the best websites for your niche and exclude the least viable within the Network, Google provides demographic and other information that will help you narrow your choices by keywords, theme, types of sites (e.g., mobile, video), areas of interest, gender, and more.

- You can then choose to view sites by Interest, Topic, Keywords, and Placements. When you select Placements, you can select individual sites by name/URL. This way you can start small by selecting only a few sites you feel are a good match for your ad(s).

Remarketing Ads. The Google Display Network gives advertisers another bite at the proverbial apple (a.k.a. interested prospects—buyers). On Bing, they're called Remessaging Ads. Here's how it works: Let's say you run a Paid Search ad with the headline, "Thinking bigger breasts?"

Suzanne, a prospective patient, Googles "breast augmentation." She sees your ad, clicks, comes to your niche website, and likes what you say about breast augmentation enough to sign up and download your free, special report, ƒ

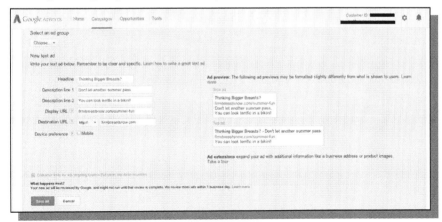

Things You Need to Ask Your Plastic Surgeon About Breast Augmentation. She's interested in you, but doesn't yet take the next step to call your office for a pre-procedural consultation.

Maybe her life is just too hectic at the moment. But she's interested. A Remarketing Ad can remind her to make a little time for herself and follow up on your offer. When Suzanne first came to your site, Google placed a cookie on her browser. That cookie triggers websites in the Display Network to show her another ad from you that reminds her about your services and may even include an inducement to act immediately. Amazon relies on Remarketing Ads to remind you of products you viewed on the Amazon website.

Now the remarketing message is very specific. Suzanne has already been to your site. She knows who you are. She doesn't need to see your original headline, "Thinking Bigger Breasts?" Instead, your Remarketing Ad headline might read: "Call Dr. Jones Today!" And the description copy might read: "Schedule beautiful breast consult. Ask about June special discounts." That's a reminder that gives her extra incentive to return to your website, get the phone number and call...before it's too late.

Remarketing Ads are a little like brand marketing, except that you can build in a Call to Action. Remember our earlier discussion? Prospects often need several contacts with you (what we call "touches") before they connect and take action. A Remarketing Ad is one way to do this. It increases the odds of a person coming back to your site and taking the next step. <u>But it's a medium-term strategy because you still need to drive that initial traffic to your website.</u>

Running the Analytics

Speaking of driving that initial traffic...

Google AdWords is not a do-it-and-forget-it process. And that's good because even the best AdWords strategists seldom "hit it out of the park" on the very first try. But it's the ability and willingness to test, track, tweak, and test some more that, in part, separates us from traditional marketers and advertisers. It's also what makes digital so powerful. You can edit, change, and tweak every aspect of your ad campaign as often as you want—even while it's running.

You can adjust your daily ad spend (up or down). Change your headline. Rewrite all or part of the copy. Add or remove keywords. Limit impressions to Exact Matches with your keyword phrase. Highlight Negative Keywords, which are the words and phrases you never want to trigger an ad impression. And more.

But you never want to make changes solely on a whim or gut instinct. That's why we use analytics, which are nothing more than metrics and statistical data presented in charts and graphs. Analytics allow you to keep your finger on the pulse of your ad campaign and website performance. The whole goal of analytics is to give you the information that will help you lower your costs while raising your clicks and conversions. You run your analytics while your ad campaign is live so that your decisions are based on actual activity. The results are real; they're not predictive or best guess. The tools provide valuable insight into how your ads are performing...but only if you know how to read the data.

Now it's possible to get very scientific about analytics and invest big dollars on third-party analytical tools. But I recommend you leave those to the professionals. Most of what you need is free and available within Google, and Google is making this easier and more useful all the time. All you really need are the analytics within Google AdWords (to measure ad performance), Google Analytics (to measure website performance) and the ability to keep office records on how many people followed up on your Call to Action by downloading your report, calling for more information, or scheduling a pre-procedure consultation, and how many became patients.

I've talked a lot about the need to optimize every aspect of your Emotional Direct Response Marketing campaign, including the niche market you choose, the website, the headline and copy, the Call to Action, and AdWords. With the help of Google Analytics and the tools and dashboards within Google AdWords, you can monitor keyword performance, number of clicks, clickthrough rates, number of impressions, average Cost Per Click, the position your ad holds on the page, even the length of time visitors spend on your website and which pages they viewed.

As with other aspects of AdWords, I can only give you a cursory introduction to analytics here. But if you want to know more, I recommend you read *Advanced Web Metrics with Google Analytics* by Brian Clifton or *Advanced Google AdWords* by Brad Geddes. These will take you in depth into the process.

So how does this work? Well, let me ask you another question: Which of the sample AdWords ads to the left will produce the most clicks and conversions? As you look at these, you'll see some obvious hints because I wrote these in very different styles, and in the second and third ads I broke several of our cardinal copywriting rules. <u>But that aside, without tracking the results, you will never know exactly what's happening and where your ad campaign is breaking down (failing).</u> Just how much testing and how granular you get is up to you and your AdWords strategist, but let me suggest a few ways you can test your ads and troubleshoot potential problems.

A/B Split Testing

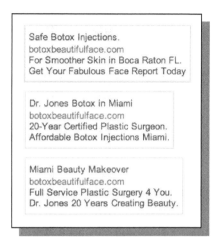

There are so many ways to test and analyze your website and AdWords data, but one of the easiest and most productive ways for you is the A/B split test. Just because you write a headline like "Safe Botox Injections" and get some traffic doesn't mean you've tapped into the best converting traffic. You may find that "Look Younger in Boca" converts twice as well. The same may be true of your descriptive copy and Display URL. And boosting your conversion rate can make a huge difference in ROI. That's why you must optimize everything.

A/B split testing allows you to create your optimal ad...the one that gets the most impressions (so you'll be seen by *buyers*) and the most clicks. Assuming your keywords target buyers, A/B split testing is cost effective because you only pay for clicks.

Here's how you run a simple A/B split test:

1. Create a campaign in AdWords and designate an Ad Group. This is important because when selecting keywords for an Ad Group, you aren't bidding on keywords for each ad separately. You eliminate the risk of bidding against yourself for the same keywords. You also level the playing field because every ad in your Ad Group uses the same keywords.

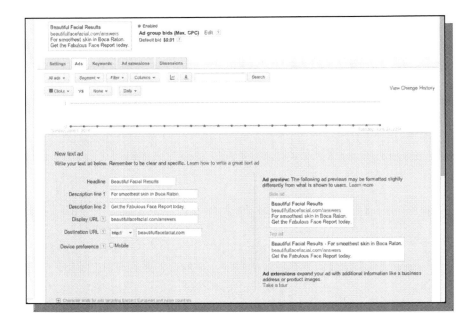

2. Write your first ad and take it live. Then write a second ad, changing only the headline. Keep the descriptive copy the same in both.

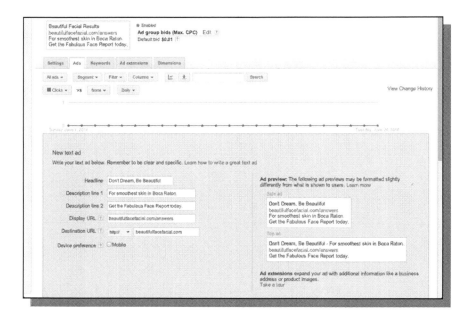

3. Take the second ad live. You now have two ads running with different headlines. Google will automatically rotate ads as long as you don't try to use any of the advanced features to optimize for conversion or clicks. All you have to do is watch the AdWords dashboard (homepage) to see which version of the ad out performs the other. How long this takes will vary based on the size of your target market and how quickly you get clicks. It could be a few days or a couple of weeks. You're looking for enough results to make your analysis statistically sound.

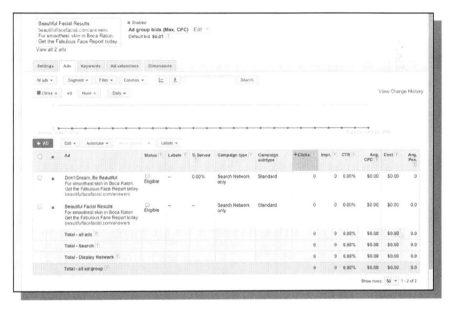

4. Once you have a winning headline, you can disable the loser and start again. Run the winner, and create a new second ad that's the same except for changes in the descriptive copy. Take it live, and wait for results.

5. If you want, you can do a third test to study your Display URL. Keep everything the same, including your URL's domain name. Test the extension (e.g., /answers).

6. You won't split test the keywords because in an Ad Group, every ad uses the same keywords. You can watch keyword

performance on your dashboard, and later you could try an advanced strategy called Conversion Tracking, which helps you identify the ads, keywords, and campaigns that are delivering the highest ROI.

7. At this point you have your first optimized ad, and it should be pulling fairly well. This is your control. But because we can always do better, create a new ad that's ENTIRELY different. Take that live, then create a third ad with a different headline than the new ad. Run through all the possibilities (outlined in steps 2-5), analyze your keyword results, and when you're done you'll have a second optimized ad.

8. For the final step, split test your first optimized ad (control) against your second optimized ad. If one consistently out pulls the other for impressions and clicks, you'll either be more confident in the viability of your control, or you'll decide to designate the second optimized ad your new control. Now if both do reasonably well, you can keep both optimized ads running. That's up to you and your AdWords strategist.

9. You can keep testing for as long as you want. Slowly, you'll be optimizing your ads for greater ROI—most impressions, most clicks, and lowest Cost Per Click. I didn't include greater conversion because that's largely a website or content issue.

Algorithms for Calculating Your Success

You'll find most of the metrics you need tracked and measured automatically on the Google AdWords is

con't

---

homepage. It's a customizable dashboard that you can layout to your own specifications, and it's comprehensive enough that you may not need to do many manual calculations. Still, it's useful to know the algorithm behind each metric. Here are some of the most common equations:

Cost Per Clicks (CPC) = Ad Spend / Clicks
Cost Per Lead (CPL) OR Cost Per Acquisition (CPA) =
Ad Spend/Conversions
Cost Per 1000 (CPM) = (Ad Spend / Impressions) X 1000
Clickthrough Rate (CTR) = (Clicks / Impressions) X 100
Conversion Rate (CR) = Conversions / Clicks
Conversions = Clicks X Conversion Rate
Return on Investment = (Profit – Cost) / Cost
Return on Ad Spend = (PPC Profit – PPC Cost) / PPC Cost

Using Analytics to Troubleshoot Your Marketing Campaigns

While A/B split testing is probably the most important component of AdWords optimization that you or your AdWords strategist will need to work on, there are other considerations and potential problems you'll need to watch for...things that can severely limit your success. These are less about testing, and more about monitoring and tracking results and understanding what the data are telling you so you can troubleshoot your campaign. Here are a few telltale metrics, what they mean, and what you can do to fix the problems:

Low # of Impressions/High Clickthrough/High Conversion: The number of impressions—which refers to how many times your ad appears in Google searches—is subjective at

145

best. What's a high number for you and your campaign, might be considered off-the-charts low for someone else with a different market or location. It can be difficult to know in the early stages of your campaign if you're getting too few impressions. That's especially true when you practice in a small city or suburban area.

The good news is that your clickthrough rate is high, which means that when your ad does appear, a high percentage of prospective patients are clicking and visiting your website. And your conversion rate is high as well, which means that a high percentage of the people visiting your website are staying long enough to read and take advantage of your Call to Action.

So that leaves the question of impressions. If you think the number of impressions may be a problem, you'll need to work on your keywords. Start testing more keywords and tracking the results.

If you feel you need some sort of benchmark of interest— any interest—in your marketing niche and community, try using a simple, short-tail keyword geo-targeted for you location. Depending on where you live, your keyword might look something like: "Botox Camden Maine" or "Breast Augmentation Orlando" or "Hair Transplants Beverly Hills." But be very careful, especially if you live in big city or high-income community where plastic surgery is in high demand. You don't want to be deluged with clicks from people who are not yet ready to become patients. Put a tight limit on your daily ad spend...maybe no more than $30 - $50 a day for a week (depending on the cost of your keywords).

Then compare results between your long-tail and short-tail keywords. If the disparity is significant, continue to test new long-tail keywords to see if you can increase impressions without reducing clickthrough or conversion percentages. In a few weeks you should have a better sense of your impressions.

High # of Impressions/Low Clickthrough/High Conversion: If your ads are getting seen, but few people seem to be clicking, you could have a couple of problems. Low clickthrough could suggest that your ad is not getting noticed or connecting with prospective patients. You may want continue split testing your headlines and copy.

The fact that you have high conversion, however, seems to indicate that at least the message or promise you're making in the ad matches well with your website. Because once someone clicks and visits your website, you're not disappointing people who come to your website (reflected in the high percentage of conversions). That's good.

Definitely test your ads, but the problem also may lie with your choices of keywords. You may not have buyer words; your ads may be coming up in the searches of too many information gatherers. In that case, the fact that your clickthrough is low could mean that your ad copy is better targeted than your keywords, which is good because even though a lot of people are seeing your ad, only the prospective patients are clicking...and they are liking what they see and read on your website because they are converting.

High # of Impressions/High Clickthrough/Low Conversion: This is NOT a place you want to be. Not only is it likely that your keywords are not targeting buyers, you're also spending too much money on clicks (high clickthrough) for little business (low conversion).

Work on your keywords to limit your ad to buyers' searches. You need better long-tail, geo-targeted keywords. You also may have a problem with your website. Is your landing page focused on your marketing niche? Are you using a strong, emotional headline and copy that connects with prospects' emotional needs? Is your Call to Action enticing, easy to access, and clearly visible on every page?

If you answered yes to all questions about the website and Call to Action, the disconnect may be between your ad and website. Even a well-written ad that doesn't set the prospect up for what you are offering on the website is, in the end, not a good ad. Don't promise what you don't deliver.

Good # of Impressions/Low Clickthrough/High Conversion: This scenario, while not wasting your money on worthless clicks, might mean that you're leaving money on the table. In other words, your website and Call to Action are working, but maybe your ad should be getting more clicks. You definitely need to test more ads. Is the problem your headline? Your description copy? That's what you need to figure out. Everything else looks good. Now see if you can increase your clickthrough rate.

Good # of Impressions/High Clickthrough/Low Conversion: This is definitely NOT a good scenario because your campaign is *costing* you too much money on clicks that don't convert. Low conversion is the same as saying you have a low ROI. The disconnect probably lies with your website and Call to Action.

In other words, your ad is getting seen, and it's connecting with prospective patients. But is it sending the right message? If the ad makes prospects believe they are getting one thing, and they get another message/offer on your website, your conversion is going to be low.

And check your website. Are you adhering to all the rules for writing a strong, niched, Emotional Direct Response website. This is a scenario you want to fix...and fast.

Good # of Impressions/High Clickthrough/High Conversion: This is your gold standard. You've achieved almost as close to perfection as possible. Continue tracking and monitoring, and if you think you can do even better, continue A/B testing your ads. But you're probably ready to start scaling your campaign.

Boosting Your Quality Score

Here's one last metric for you to think about. I mentioned Quality Score (QS) earlier in this chapter. It's important because Google sets your QS and uses it to determine the price you'll pay for keywords and your position on the search page. You want to keep your Cost Per Click as low as possible and your Page Position as high as possible.

Note: Your Quality Score is measured on each keyword. A perfect QS is 10. You may have a QS of 10 for one keyword and a QS of five for another. Once you take a campaign live, you can find your QS metric tied to the keywords in your campaign.

Although Google keeps its algorithm a secret, we do know a few things that Google is measuring. Your Quality Score is, in part, the aggregate of 1) the number of times your keywords match a search query, 2) the relevance of your keywords and ads (measured by your clickthrough rate), 3) quality of the content on your website and landing page, 4) amount of time visitors spend on your site (Google Analytics will give you this information), 5) ad performance relative to others in your content area and geographical region who are using the same keyword, and 6) landing page load time, which is why you should avoid lots of big graphics, Flash, and videos that take a long time to load.

Here's a simplified algorithm for calculating QS:

$$\text{Quality Score} = \text{Relevance (Keywords + Ads + URL)} + \text{User Experience}$$

LESSON FOUR—START SMALL THEN SCALE:
Because you're using Paid Search, you can't afford to
get it wrong. Well, you can, but only if you start small.
And that means limiting your financial exposure. Set a
budget for the amount of money you want to spend
each day on ad clicks—something you can afford to
lose as you're testing and optimizing. When you are
getting the results you want, it's time to scale up.

Scaling Your Paid Search Campaigns

At the beginning of this chapter, I mentioned that both Paid and Owned media are scalable. Let me explain what I mean. Scaling is about momentum and being able to take your initial, small results and replicating them on a larger scale. In the case of Paid media, once you can generate good traffic and earn a solid ROI—consistently and reliably—you should be able to increase your ad spend and enjoy the same results.

If you spend $200 monthly for a consistent 20 percent clickthrough rate and a 68 percent conversion rate (number of prospects that respond to your Call to Action), then spending $2000 a month should yield about the same percentages of clicks and conversions. And if you closed, say $8,000 of new business for every $200 spent, then you should bring in roughly $80,000 of new business for every $2000 spent.

> Scaling is about momentum and
> being able to take your initial, small
> results and replicating them on a
> larger scale.

That's scalability...in theory. And in fact, it holds up pretty well for a national or global Internet marketing campaign selling digital products and membership services. It's how I scaled my hypnosis business to a $20,000 a month ad spend and brought in at least double that amount in sales month after month. Of course, I didn't launch my business with $20,000 a month in PPC ads. I gradually scaled up. And I didn't scale up to a $200,000 monthly ad spend to close $400,000 worth of business because there is a point of diminishing returns. There wasn't a large-enough market to generate $400,000 worth of business each month; $40,000 in monthly revenue turned out to be my sweet spot.

Now, when selling professional services and medical procedures locally—as is your case—the size of your market and its demand for plastic surgery will impact your scalability. For example, in large, high-income cities like New York, LA/Hollywood, Boca Raton/Miami, San Francisco/Silicon Valley, Scottsdale/Phoenix, Las Vegas and Northern Virginia/DC, your AdWords campaigns should scale easily. These locations have both the population and demand to grow with your ad spend.

On the other hand, while Bar Harbor, Maine; McCall, Idaho; and Jackson Hole, Wyoming—all upscale resort communities—have the money, they lack the population density to scale as dramatically. Eventually, every campaign will reach a point of diminishing returns where sales can no longer scale on par with investment, and some practices will hit their sweet spot more quickly than others. This is another reason to track your analytics carefully.

So how quickly can you begin scaling your AdWords campaign? That's easy...it varies. Seriously, you can only begin scaling when you see a solidly profitable ROI on your small investment. Sometimes you can start a campaign and within 30-to-45 days be booking new patients for procedures. Conversely, it could be 60-90-120 days before you're getting a good ROI that you want to scale. Regardless of how long it takes, I suggest you stay small for a couple more months, just to ensure that you have consistent, reliable results.

And I have to say that working with a professional who knows how to build, run and manage an Emotional Direct Response Marketing campaign will get you to your goal faster. We all learn to build and market Paid Search campaigns the same way—through trial and error. Yes, we've all made mistakes early in our careers. But when you work with professionals, they've already learned the hard lessons. You get the benefit of our experience.

Scaling Your Owned Media

So that's just about everything you need to know to understand how an Emotional Direct Response Marketing campaign works. But before closing this chapter and turning to the Conclusion, I want to address one more aspect of your marketing strategy. And that's Owned media, which includes social media, blogging and Search Engine Optimization (SEO). I'm including it as part of our discussion on scaling because it represents an expansion (or scaling) of your marketing program, and you really shouldn't attempt it until your Paid Search (and possibly even your Display Network and Remarketing advertising) are running smoothly and delivering a good return on investment.

I know there's a lot of buzz about social media (e.g., Facebook, Twitter, Pinterest, Instagram, etc.) and blogging. Strategies and tactics abound. I don't have a lot I want to include here because that's a whole other book. Instead I will refer you to a few books: *Likeable Social Media* by Dave Kerpen, *Social Media ROI* by Olivier Blanchard, *The Zen of Social Media*

Marketing by Shama Kabani, *My Blog Traffic Sucks* by Steve Scott, and *Expert Briefs: Blogging for Profit* by Nicole Dean.

What I do want to share with you is my perspective on how social media and blogging fit into an Emotional Direct Response Marketing strategy. Emotional Direct Response Marketing using Paid Search is a short-term strategy. With professional help, you can be getting new patients and making a reasonable return on your investment in a few short months. And you can literally buy your way onto the first page of Google searches that target prospective patients in your area who are most likely to be ready to move forward with selecting a plastic surgeon. That's not the case with blogging and social media.

Blogging. Blogging is, at best, a medium-term strategy. I know one author who advises her writing clients to start blogging the same day they decide to write a book because it can take that long to get established with an audience of regular readers and reach the first page of Google as a non-paid, organic entry.

Understanding SEO is as critical to your blogging success as writing good content week after week after week. But Google is forever changing the algorithm for organic SEO, which means that one day you can be on page one of Google only to drop to page 10 the next...literally. I've heard that Google makes some 700-odd algorithm changes a year, which works out to about two a day. And you have to keep up with that—to reach (and remain on) page one of Google.

Still, 100s (maybe even 1000s) of people make a living blogging, and 1000s more swear by blogging. There's no question that the more ways you have to connect with a prospective patient (a.k.a. touches) the better. But I'll also tell you that many of the top AdWords advertisers either don't blog or relegate it to an occasional activity.

If you do decide to make blogging part of your medium- to long-term strategy, use WordPress—the same platform you're using for your niche website. It's user-friendly, easy to use, the search engines love it, and for $100 or so, you can hire someone to design your site and set you up with a hosting company. By reading any book about blogging, you can learn about title tags, meta tags, your description and all the elements that boost your blog's SEO capability.

If you're looking for a secondary marketing strategy to augment your Emotional Direct Response Marketing, I can tell you that *Search Engine Journal* reports that SEO leads generated through blogging and other online strategies have a 14.6 percent close rate versus outbound marketing leads generated through print advertising and traditional direct mail (1.7 percent close rate). So that's something to think about. And if you can capture one of the top positions for organic search entries—and maintain your position—you will receive a lot of clicks. It's what makes blogging a viable medium- to long-term strategy.

Social Media. These days, social media is the big buzzword. But I need to dispel some of the myths about social media. **First**, it's not the second coming; it's just another way to connect with potential patients. And **second**, connecting with the people in your area most likely to want the plastic surgery procedure you're promoting in your AdWords campaign (your niche market) is tricky and not nearly as straightforward as you might think.

There's a reason it's called "social" media. I heard this analogy from Internet marketer Perry Belcher, and it's a brilliant analogy: Social media is like going into a bar with your friends and hanging out. You're talking about this and that, and a stranger walks up to you and says, "Hi, my name is Joe Smith, and I'm a plastic surgeon. I can give you a great head of hair that will make you look 20 years younger." Now Dr. Smith may actually be able

154

to deliver on his promise, but socially what he just did is completely inappropriate. He isn't one of your drinking buddies; he's a total stranger. He didn't make a friendly introduction; he didn't even offer to buy you a beer before launching into his spiel.

Social media works much the same way. You can't just create a Facebook Page or open a Twitter account and start promoting your services. Even using an emotional pitch won't work. You have to hang out, build rapport, and talk socially. Anything else and you're interrupting people and imposing on their fun time. Facebook is a social gathering, and if you're going to break in and build Friends and Likes, you need to create a social gathering of your own. But it won't be by constantly talking about plastic surgery or breast augmentations or Botox or hair transplantations. You have to be social in social media.

So why would somebody want to visit your Facebook Page, Pinterest or Instagram site? Because you're talking about something that interests your target market. If your marketing niche is hair transplantation for men, you could talk sports...Miami Heat, LA Dodgers, Chicago Bulls. If you're into sports—and I'm not, so this would be a difficult strategy for me—talk about your local sports teams. Other topics could be local, newsworthy events. If your niche is Botox treatments and you want to reach women in their late 40s and up, you could talk about charity events in Boca Raton, movie premiers, local art exhibits—something that you can talk intelligently about (if you're a man) that appeals to women of a certain age.

If you want to promote breast augmentation surgery, maybe you focus on the local beach scene. If you're a woman, you could build a following discussing women's clothing trends, fashion designers, sexy new looks, etc. Every niche will require content and conversation tailored to the demographics and psychographics of your target market. Hobbies (e.g., painting, reading, music, etc.) and personal sports (e.g., golf, kayaking, kickboxing, tennis, etc.) are also good subjects that you can tie to target markets.

Does it work? Yes. Does Google like you to use social media? Absolutely. It demonstrates evidence of your social authority, and there's an algorithm for that too. If you can make your posts and comments interesting and relevant, and you keep up the conversation for the long haul, in time you can interject a few references to your practice and what you are marketing. Once you've made the leap, and your Friends and Followers (what marketer Dan Kennedy calls a Herd and Seth Godin calls a Tribe) accept your subject, you can share news of special offers you're running and where to go to download your special report. But keep it subtle and unobtrusive. To make social media work for your practice will take time and creativity. It's a long-term strategy you should plan for but not implement until your Paid Search is up, running and successful.

Scaling Your Website with SEO

Throughout this book we've focused on the niche website you need in order to mount an effective Emotional Direct Response Marketing campaign. For effectiveness, it supplants the generic, cover-the-waterfront types of websites that retailers, service providers, and professional practices typically use to build their businesses. As we've discussed, even the best of these one-size-fits-all websites cannot be optimized for a direct response campaign that uses Paid Search to drive traffic. They're just too general.

That said, I'm not naïve enough to believe that all those traditional websites are going to go away in favor of niche sites. And that's okay. In fact, what you should do is incorporate your generic websites into your marketing strategy as a form of long-term brand and image building. They're not going to build your practice in the short term the way Paid Search will. And that's why I've saved my explanation of search engine optimization (SEO) for this section on scaling. Website SEO is about trying to get your site into one of the top non-paid, organic positions on the first page of Google or Bing or any other search engine, but it's not going to happen overnight. It can take months and maybe a year or more to gain prominence in organic search.

SEO is a complex process that requires a good design, engaging copy, a smart strategy, and constant attention. It's also not inexpensive. Businesses that set up and maintain websites for SEO can charge $650 a month and more to help you reach your goal. **So my advice is this:** When you are ready to focus on SEO, you first evaluate the effectiveness of your generic website. For example, if it's just another run-of-the-mill site that puts too much emphasis on the physicians and the clinic up front, and doesn't speak to prospective patients, you need to redesign and rewrite it using many of the techniques we discussed in Chapter 3. Every good website needs to make an emotional connection with people.

The SEO algorithms Google and other search engines use today for evaluating websites are complex and forever changing. Only a few years ago, keywords—embedded in a site's title tags, meta tags and descriptions and sprinkled liberally throughout the copy—were about all you needed to get to page one. But the practice was abused. So in it's effort to thwart people who gamed the system (by placing more importance on their SEO strategy than on the quality of their content), Google redesigned its algorithms to include metrics for measuring the quality of content, number and quality of backlinks, social authority, and more. And Google is forever revising its algorithms. SEO, today, is a moving target, which is why you need the help of an SEO professional.

I'm going to give you a brief overview of some of these SEO metrics. But first, let me say that these strategies will work not only on your generic website and blog but also on your niche websites. There's no reason your niche sites can't place high among the non-paid, organic search results. In fact, it's an excellent strategy that will pay off in the long run. It's also challenging, as you're about to see:

Keywords. Keywords are still an essential part of your on-site or on-page SEO strategy. During the site's set up, you need to embed your best long-tail keywords (and they should be buyer words) in your site's title, meta tags, and description. Google scans the site's HTML source code looking for the keywords.

The best way to understand this is for me to show you how the source code correlates to what you see on the website. I Googled "breast augmentation new york," and here's the first page from that search:

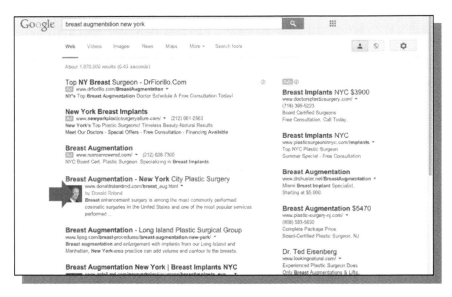

I clicked on the first organic entry, and when the site opened I clicked on VIEW in my browser bar, then selected VIEW SOURCE from the dropdown menu. You can try this yourself (although the technique for viewing source code may vary depending on your browser), and a separate window will open showing you the HTML code.

As you scroll through the source code, you'll find the embedded keywords:

<title>New York City Breast Augmentation | Breast Enhancement New York</title>

<meta name="keywords" content="breast augmentation,breast lift,breast reconstruction,breast reduction,cosmetic surgery,plastic surgery" />

<meta name="description" content="Breast enhancement surgery...New York." />

(**Note:** I added the ellipses in the description code above to conserve space. The description is used to describe the site in the search entry.)

Content. Now, there's more you can do with keywords. You can use them in your copy, but (and this is important) do so judiciously. If you just start cramming your copy with keywords (what's called "keyword stuffing") you will negatively impact your SEO. Google doesn't like that. By all means use your keywords, but use them as part of your effort to write strong, emotional copy that connects with readers.

As part of Google's effort to reward good websites with top positions in organic search results, Google measures the *user experience.* Just as you can use Google Analytics to track the number of users on your site, how they came to your site, the number of pages they viewed, and how long they spent reading, Google is doing the same thing, and they know when poorly written copy is stuffed with keywords and fails to hold reader attention.

When you're counting on SEO to boost your website in organic search, you face a bit of a balancing act between keywords and strong, emotional copy. You have two masters: Google and your prospective patients.

In this respect, it's easier to write copy for your niche website as part of an Emotional Direct Response Marketing campaign because SEO is not your primary concern. Your number one objective is to connect with readers using a strong, emotional message that compels prospective patients to take the next step with you. Then you select buyer keywords as part of your AdWords campaign to drive good, highly targeted traffic to your niche website. In a website SEO strategy, you're trying to use your keywords effectively while also trying to write compelling copy.

Backlinks. As part of its effort to identify sites that deliver a strong user experience, Google tracks the number of other websites that link to your website. These are called "inbound links" or "backlinks." And not any backlinks, either. Google is looking for Authority, and the more authoritative the linking sites are rated, the higher your own Authority will be. Authority equals user experience.

The metric for Authority is Page Rank. On a scale of 1 to 10, CNN.com and NYtimes.com both have Page Ranks of 9/10; WhiteHouse.gov has a Page Rank of 10/10. These are sites people spend a long time on—reading and researching subjects—and that's evidence of a good user experience.

In the offline world, we can equate Authority with, among others, our religious leaders, top physicians, top accountants, and top legal counsel. In each case, when we have a question—be it moral, medical, financial, or legal—we seek the opinion and/or advice of a person with high authority. And we give their advice a lot of weight. They've earned our trust. Google does much the same thing, and they assign Authority with a high Page Rank. The higher a website's Page Rank is, the higher its position in search. And the more backlinks you have from high-ranking sites, the higher you will rank in search.

Your challenge is to get backlinks from these Authority sites. One way you can do this is to send out press releases. Let's say you put out the word that you wrote a book entitled *Hollywood's Best Facelift Secrets*, and the Authority site CNN.com picks up your story. CNN.com will include a link to your website in its story; that's a backlink with Authority. The more of these you have, the higher you'll rank.

By the way, you can check your website (or any other website's) Page Rank. There are many free tool sites available; to find one just search for "Page Rank tool."

Social Authority. Finally, you want evidence of your social authority to help boost your SEO. Now this also is about links, but it's a little different from Page Rank Authority. Social authority tells Google that users like your website or blog post, which simply means that people are talking about you and linking to you on the social sites—Facebook, Twitter, Pinterest, Instagram, etc. It's very grassroots. Think word of mouth...digital style. Google sees that you're generating interest, so your user experience must be pretty good. You're not scamming the system or being overly salesy, you're just generating a lot of buzz, which Google likes to see.

What you can do to generate social authority is start people talking by posting about your website or latest blog post on the social sites and include a link back to your website. If people like what you're saying, they'll Share your news with their own Friends and Followers. They'll Like what you're saying. Or they'll Re-Tweet your message on Twitter.

And that's a little insight into SEO. It's good, but it's definitely a long-term strategy. It's branding, and as with any branding strategy, it's impossible to target buyers. You can get a lot of traffic, but it's not

> So in the short term, spend your money building a niche website, buying keywords (good buyer keywords), hiring an Emotional Direct Response Marketing strategist, and getting money coming in.

necessarily all good traffic. You're going to reach people at all stages of the research and buying process—from information gatherers to people who are actively looking for a physician. You'll need a sales funnel strategy with plenty of ways to nurture these leads, and that includes free reports, email campaigns, and

Remarketing Ads. Much of your SEO-generated traffic will require many more "touches" before you have a chance of converting them into patients. It's a long sales cycle.

So in the short term, spend your money building a niche website, buying keywords (good buyer keywords), hiring an Emotional Direct Response Marketing strategist, and getting money coming in. Then, if you want, take some of your profits and invest in scaling up your marketing strategy to include blogging, social media and SEO.

I'll leave you with this: I said that these medium- to long-term strategies can generate business. I want to mention Toyota of Hollywood (in the Miami area). This local auto dealership generates a lot of business through Facebook. They have more than 14,000 Likes, and they've put their name out there so much and so many people have Googled the dealership, that Toyota of Hollywood is now an official keyword. It gets on average about 12,000 searches per month and has a suggested bid price of about $1.50. It has cost the dealership a lot of money to accomplish this and to build their Facebook presence, but it's a huge branding success. It's branding; they didn't build their presence with direct response and AdWords buys. That said, they do now run AdWords ads, as you'll see if you Google Toyota of Hollywood.

But here's the kicker, other dealerships are able to buy the "Toyota of Hollywood" keyword too, and they are coming up on the first page of search queries for Toyota of Hollywood. And that's not a bad strategy. They're getting the benefits without the tremendous investment in time and money that Toyota of Hollywood has had to make. Proof, again, that Paid Search is still your best short-term strategy.

And that's it. You now have a good overview of what it takes to develop a Kick-Ass Emotional Direct Response

Marketing campaign. What's your next step? That's what we'll address in the Conclusion.

Chapter 5
Take the Next Step!
Invest in Your Success!

*"Search engine marketing and search
engine optimization are critically
important to online businesses. You
can spend every penny you have on a
website, but it will all be for nothing
if nobody knows your site is there."*

– *Marc Ostrofsky, entrepreneur/venture capitalist*

Are you ready to make this the year you really put the
Internet to work building your practice? Will you join
the growing ranks of forward-thinking marketers who
understand how to channel the true power of the Internet?

Now truly is the best time to act. As more and more
marketers learn to use Paid Search effectively and begin to create
better, more compelling ads, even more end users and prospects

(buyers) are reading and clicking on highly targeted, well-written ads that speak to them. The proof is in the statistics. Digital marketing technology firm, IgnitionOne, reports that in Q4 2013 clickthrough rates for Paid Search rose 25 percent year over year. And the momentum continues: Los Angeles-based The Search Agency confirms that in Q1 2014 clickthrough rates grew 10 percent year over year.

If you are ready to move forward, you have one critical decision to make today: to do it yourself or work with a professional strategist. I want you to be inspired by what you can achieve with an Emotional Response Direct Marketing campaign. I want you to know the right questions to ask of your vendors and service providers. I want you to recognize a good campaign from just another mediocre example of incestuous marketing. But I don't want to give you a false sense of confidence. We have only brushed the surface of what you need to do. It takes years of study and work and, yes, even mistakes to know how to design highly optimized websites, write copy like a pro, and build an AdWords campaign that delivers prospective patients ready to make a buying decision.

And one more thing: Like any growing industry, Paid Search continues to mature as marketers become more sophisticated and Google, Bing and other Search platforms add more features, advanced options, and new ad formats (e.g., audience-based search options and industry-specific ad formats). For example, Google's Enhanced Campaigns now enables you to more accurately target your prospects' search interests. And more and better features for Product Listing Ads and Remarketing Ads make these increasingly serious contenders for your ad dollars. But it's hard to keep up on best practices if you're busy managing your practice and performing surgery.

It boils down to what level of involvement you want. I know that a few of you will read this book and decide to jump in and build your own site, write your own copy, and run your own AdWords campaigns. Some of you will assign the task to staff. And there are those among you who will try to hire and manage a team of freelance designers, writers, and advertising specialists. I wish you well. A few of you will succeed although the learning curve may be painful.

Invest in Your Success

For those of you who hire a strategic consultant, the path to success will be faster and more affordable than you think. While I recommend outsourcing your Emotional Direct Response Marketing campaign to a strategic consultant, beware the marketing professional brandishing a few awards and a sample book full of brochures, postcards, white papers, DVDs, and tear sheets from previous projects. They may have top-notch designers and gifted writers on staff, but if they can't demonstrate that they understand how to build a strategy that delivers return on your investment—RUN.

Remember my beef with the media buyer who prided herself on her agency's ability to deliver "eyeballs?" Well, eyeballs are not patients; they're not even prospects. And eyeballs don't quickly or easily translate into sales.

Most agencies will trot out the color chart and suggest a new look; they'll give you a brochure, a fancy new logo, a website with all the bells and whistles, a radio or TV spot, or a full-color print ad. But these are only things...what marketers call deliverables. You think you need a brochure; they'll deliver a brochure. You want greater online presence; they'll create a Facebook Page, a Twitter account, or a blog. You ask for an AdWords campaign; they'll say, "sure."

Most agencies and traditional marketers will try to make you happy through deference and flattery. They'll cater to your opinion but ignore the most obvious way to make you happy...by delivering results. Tell them you want a return on your investment and see what happens. All eyes may be on you, but the look is pure deer in the headlights.

You need a strategy for success—short-term success. And only an Emotional Direct Response Marketing strategist can develop a complete sales campaign—from strategy to tactics, market to media, and website to traffic. If you're going to invest in building your practice, bringing in new patients, and positioning yourself above the field, then work with someone who has his or her eye on *your* bottom line.

Should you buy a $7 keyword? Can your clickthrough rate be higher? Should you expect more impressions? Is it time to scale up? Is it time to move into social media? Is your sales funnel working? Are conversions where they should be? These are the kinds of questions only a strategic consultant can answer with the kind of authority that comes from experience, the willingness to track results, and a full hands-on approach to meeting your objectives.

And research. A successful marketing campaign does not run on gut instinct and guesswork. It is the product of knowledge and insight...knowledge about your profession, your market, and optimization techniques, and insight from the data generated and analyzed as the campaign is running.

This last component is essential; it's the reason a marketing strategist's job does not end when the Paid Search ads are up and running. A true strategist will optimize a campaign's components and diagnose any problems with an eye to continually increasing your return on invest.

Invest in your success; anything less is failure. This book will help you know when you've found the person who can deliver.

On that note, let me explain how I work.

Working with Marc Savage

If you work with me, I start with your input. I want to understand your practice so I can help you define your niche market and focus your objectives for growing the practice. This is not a general consult. It's a full-out brain dump. This is where together we dig in and dig deep to get specific. I want to know the wants and desires and demographics of your patients. How your sales process typically works. Your areas of specialization. And if it can be arranged, I'd like to meet a typical patient, and I'll sign a non-disclosure if necessary.

> My success metrics are based on me performing to the best of my ability to deliver results...And your success metrics are tied to mine...

After our initial meeting, your day-to-day involvement is minimal. I'll show you the website; you'll give me your feedback and tell me if there's anything that makes you uncomfortable. If you have any concerns, we'll discuss them. If your points are valid, I'm okay with removing something. But I require final say on the marketing approach—outside of doing something that's illegal for a plastic surgeon and could result in a lawsuit. And I have this in writing in my client agreements.

My success metrics are based on me performing to the best of my ability to deliver results, so I require the latitude to do what my experience tells me works. And your success metrics are tied to mine, so it's in your best interest to listen to me.

The truth is, if a client tries to micro-manage what is my area of expertise, I'd probably charge more for the headaches and extra work involved. As a physician, I think you can understand where I'm coming from. You discuss what a patient wants, but you don't hand over a scalpel and invite him or her to assist in the surgery.

Once we launch the campaign, your office is going to handle the phone calls. It's important that whomever takes the initial call asks if the website Call to Action and/or your report prompted the caller to take action. We can also set up the Call to Action so that when prospective patients contact your office, they are encouraged to frame their request in a certain way. We can tell them to call and say, "I want your Beautiful Breast survey" or "I want to schedule a Younger, Thicker Hair session." And I'll work with you on how to do that.

Although your involvement in implementing the marketing is minimal, you're never out of the loop. It's my job to make the program work—from end to end. But when the campaign goes live, I will report to you on the campaign analytics. And you're going to tell me how many phone calls you receive, how many meetings are scheduled, how many procedures are booked, etc. This way, we'll both know how the campaign is performing, what components need fine-tuning, and when it's time to start scaling the campaign for growth.

I don't manage Paid Search campaigns for clients. What I do is manage your marketing campaign. The big picture, and that's a critical distinction. Based on our initial meeting, I provide the market research, set the message with just the right emotional tone, and I oversee every element of the AdWords campaign.

I also write website copy—sales letters for landing pages, direct mail, and headlines are my specialties. And I manage the creative process. I have top people who design websites as well as write special reports and ad copy. But before a campaign goes live, every element must meet my rigorous standards and adhere to the trilogy of Market-Message-Media.

I also have experienced professionals who develop, monitor, test, and track AdWord campaigns. While I leave the traffic management and analysis to the specialists, I research and manage the keyword selection process. It's the critical component of every campaign. If your ads are not getting in front of the right traffic—buyers—the best ad copy in the world can't save you.

I spend a lot of time in the early phases of a marketing campaign thoroughly researching markets and keywords. I've gotten very good at thinking like a buyer (in this case, like your prospective patient). I get inside their heads to understand their motivation. I like to create an avatar, of sorts, for a typical buyer in a market niche, which I define according to that buyer's physical characteristics, demographic data, and psychographic behavior. By the time I'm ready to write copy, I can see, hear, and think like your buyer. I know where he or she hangs out online, publications read, concerns, desires, issues, and what he or she wants in a product or service.

Anyone can write some copy, scrape a bunch of keywords, throw up a website and launch a marketing campaign. Most of the time these campaigns fail. (Maybe you've had this experience) I work with specific people in mind.

Now it's your turn. I invite you to take action today. Call me at 561-544-7995. We'll schedule a time to discuss how you can build your practice with more profitable surgeries every month— delivered with autopilot consistency.

Made in the USA
Charleston, SC
19 July 2014